A History
of the Red Dragon

by
Carl Lofmark

Edited by G.A. Wells

No. 4
WELSH HERITAGE SERIES

GWASG Carreg Gwalch

ISBN: 0-86381-317-8

*First published in 1995 by Gwasg Carreg Gwalch,
Iard yr Orsaf, Llanrwst, Gwynedd, Wales.*
☎ (01492) 642031

Printed and published in Wales.

Contents

Editor's Preface

When Carl Lofmark died, tragically prematurely, in October 1991, he had almost succeeded in completing this booklet, at which he had been working during his brave three-year struggle with cancer. His interest in the subject goes back many years, and is apparent in his closely argued article of 1976 on the Red Dragon of Wales ('Der rote Drache der Waliser'), published at Vienna in a 'Festschrift' for the distinguished Austrian mediaeval scholar Otto Höfler (*Philologia Germanica*, volume 3, edited by Helmut Birkhan).

Lofmark came to Lampeter from his lectureship at King's College, London, in 1964, as founder of the German Department at St. David's College, and was appointed Professor there when the Chair was instituted ten years later. Every graduate in German there has been taught by him — he was still teaching within days of his death — and a very large number of them have written to express their sadness at his death. As a keen and sympathetic student of things Welsh, he wanted to expand his 1976 article and make its substance available in English to readers in Great Britain. He had already published an introduction to Old Welsh poetry under the title *Bards and Heroes* (Llanerch, 1989), and the warm encouragement he experienced from his colleagues in Celtic studies made him all the readier for the new task.

I have done no more to the manuscript of my late colleague and close friend than check and complete the references, make what corrections are necessary, and — in the case of the final chapter — spell out his notes into a continuous text. A little of the mortar is mine, but all the bricks are certainly his. I gratefully acknowledge the help I have received from his widow, Mrs Maureen Lofmark, and from Dr Dafydd Evans of St. David's University College. I am grateful too to my former secretary, Mrs Evelyn Stone, for her continued readiness in retirement to type manuscripts for me, including this one.

I hope that this booklet will find acceptance as a fitting final achievement of a fine scholar and much-loved teacher. Any proceeds from its sale will help to fund the Carl Lofmark Scholarship for students of German or Swedish in the Department he set up in 1964 at Saint David's University College, Lampeter.

Abbreviations Used for References in Text and Notes

Allen and Griffiths: Judy Allen and Jeanne Griffiths, *The Book of the Dragon*, (London, 1979)

Anglo (1961): Sidney Anglo, The *'British History* in Early Tudor Propaganda', *Bulletin of the John Rylands Library*, 44 (1961-62) 17-48

Anglo (1969): Sidney Anglo, *Spectacle, Pageantry and Early Tudor Policy*, (Oxford 1969)

Barber and Riches: R. Barber and A. Riches, *A Dictionary of Fabulous Beasts*, (London, 1971)

Bromwich: Rachel Bromwich, *Trioedd Ynys Prydein*, (Cardiff, 1961)

Elliott Smith: G. Elliott Smith, *The Evolution of the Dragon*, (Manchester, 1919)

H.T. Evans: Howell T. Evans, *Wales and the Wars of the Roses*, (Cambridge, 1915)

Fontenrose: J. Fontenrose, *Python. A Study of Delphic Myth and Its Origins*,(Berkeley/Los Angeles, 1959)

Garmon Jones: W. Garmon Jones, 'Welsh Nationalism and Henry Tudor',*TSC*, 1917-18, 1-59.

GPC: Geiriadur Prifysgol Cymru, vol. 1, (Cardiff, 1967)

Griffiths: Margaret Enid Griffiths, *Early Vaticination in Welsh*, edited by T. Gwynn Jones, Cardiff, 1937.

Gwynn Jones: T. Gwynn Jones, *Welsh Folk-Lore and Folk-Custom*, (London 1930)

Haverfield and Macdonald: F. Haverfield and G. Macdonald, *The Roman Occupation of Britain*, (Oxford, 1924)

Huxley: Francis Huxley, *The Dragon*, (London, 1979)

Ingersoll: Ernest Ingersoll, *Dragons and Dragon Lore*, (New York, 1928)

F. Jones: Francis Jones, *The Princes and Principalities of Wales*, (Cardiff, 1969)

Kendrick: T.D. Kendrick, *British Antiquity*, (London, 1950)

Pauly-Wissowa: Pauly-Wissowa, *Real-Encyclopädie der Classischen Altertumswissenschaft*

Sälzle: K. Sälzle, *Tier und Mensch. Gottheit und Demon*, (München, 1965)

Schramm: P.E. Schramm, *Herrschaftszeichen und Staatssymbolik: Schriften der Monumenta Germaniae Historica*, 13 (part 2), (Stuttgart, 1955)

Simpson: Jacqueline Simpson, *British Dragons*, (London, 1980)

Tatlock: J.S.P. Tatlock, 'The Dragons of Wessex and Wales', *Speculum 8* (1933), 223-235

Topsell: Edward Topsell, *The History of Serpents*, forming vol. 2 of his *The History of Four-Footed Beasts and Serpents and Insects*, (London, 1658; reprinted New York, 1967)

Trevelyan: Marie Trevelyan, *Folk-Lore and Folk Stories of Wales*, (London, 1909)

TSC: Transactions of the Honourable Society of Cymmrodorion

Visser: M.W. de Visser, *The Dragon in China and Japan*, Amsterdam, 1913 (*Verhandelingen der Koninklijke Akademie van Wetenschappen te Amsterdam*, (13 [2] 1-237)

Wild (1962): Friedrich Wild, 'Drachen im Beowulf und andere Drachen', *Osterreichische Akademie der Wissenschaften*, phil.-hist. Klasse, Sitzungsberichte, vol. 238 (essay no. 5), (Vienna, 1962), 1-56

Wild (1963): Friedrich Wild, 'Der Drache als englisches Königssymbol', *Anzeiger der österreichischen Akademie der Wissenschaften*, phil.-hist. Klasse, vol. 100 (1963), 93-103

PROFFWYDOLIAETH MYRDDIN

A poster illustrating Myrddin's prophecy — the defeat
of the white dragon on the claws of the red dragon.

Chapter 1

The Dragon in Prehistory and in Ancient History

(i) The Origin of the Dragon and his Relation to Real Animals

The first dragons were created many thousands of years ago in the imagination of archaic man. Some of their features were probably copied from real animals, which therefore resemble the dragon in one way or another; but the dragon itself never existed anywhere on earth except in the minds of our early ancestors, as a focus for their fears, their piety and their imagination.

Among the real inhabitants of this world which the dragon in some way resembles are the snakes, lizards and crocodiles. One such creature is a large monitor lizard known as the Komodo dragon, living in Indonesia (Figure 1). The largest adults of this species weigh about 135 kilograms (300 pounds), are three meters (about ten feet) long, and may live to be a hundred.[1] But though this creature is called a dragon, it is in fact only an outsize lizard. Its habitat is restricted to a few islands in a remote corner of the orient and its existence appears to have been unknown to all except the islanders until the present century. On closer inspection, this creature — which is wingless — is more like the crocodile than the dragon and, apart from its size, it differs very little from other lizards. It is only in the imagination of its modern discoverers that it has become associated with the dragon of ancient and mediaeval myth.

There are also large serpents which resemble some of the archaic and oriental representations of the dragon, which have a serpentine form, and there are creatures of the sea, such as giant squids and large eels, which may bring the dragon to mind. But these, too, are clearly not dragons in fact.

Given the enormous variety of species known and the various conceptions of the dragon's form and nature, it is inevitable that one or other of nature's real animals will in some way resemble some version of the dragon. But each of them, on closer inspection, can be identified quite definitely as something else. The dragon himself is a creature of fantasy.

* * *

Businesses, shops, agencies — even whole cities
use the dragon logo with fervour

But although he never lived anywhere on earth as a real animal, the dragon has lived everywhere in the human mind, indeed he has been a familiar and important beast in the imagination of the entire human race over many thousands of years. From the earliest times mankind has always been very much aware of his existence, and the record goes back deep into prehistory. Everywhere, from Europe and the Near East to India and China, in all of Africa, in both North and South America and the Pacific Islands, including prehistoric Australia and New Zealand, the dragon always played a large part in myth and religion and he was always greatly feared, from the first records of humanity until a mere century or so ago.[2]

Across five continents and over many thousands of years people have differed in their view of his attributes and form — the variants range from those of the orient and our own archaic past, which show him as a long serpentine creature of the clouds, down to the big bad beast of the mediaeval west, where he is rather more like an ordinary quadruped and usually lives on the ground, in barren places and dark caves. But this range of variation is small when we consider the general consistency of the dragon's image in very different places and among very different peoples. Despite local differences of form and function, the dragon was always an enormous reptilian monster, thick skinned and scaly; he mostly possessed wings (except in China and Japan where, although he was a creature of the air, he often managed without them).[3] In most cases he had legs, and there was a tail, often pointed; and he breathed fire, though he might live in clouds or water. Everywhere he was formidable, whether as an ally to man, as in China, or as man's enemy, as elsewhere. He might in some ways resemble the crocodile, the griffin or the salamander, but he was never confused with them. His general appearance was universally well known and his identity was clear. Our ancestors knew well which beast they meant when they spoke of the dragon.

* * *

Through all those thousands of years when the dragon was a potent force in the imagination of all peoples there was never any serious doubt about his real existence. Archaic and mediaeval people were predisposed to believe many things which they could not know from their own limited experience and had no means to test, and which they therefore had to take on trust. People who have never seen a crocodile, a salamander, a griffin, a dragon or an elephant had no good reason to suppose that some of these

DRAGONS

ISSUE 26 JANUARY 1995

The Football Association of Wales

Cymde Bêl Droed Cymru

NORTH WALES it's magic

Tourist Information Centres

Use the Wales Tourist Board's network of TICs when you're on your travels. TICs provide information on what to see and where to go, scenic routes and local events. They also operate a handy bed-booking service and stock a comprehensive range of tourist literature. All TICs are open from April to September. The following, which remain open throughout the year, will be happy to provide further information if you're planning a visit.

On the sporting fields and in the tourist trade, the dragon of Wales always makes its presence felt.

THE RETURN OF THE DRAGON
Welsh Triple Crown Victory 1988

A BBC TV SPORTS PRESENTATION

beasts were fabulous and others real, and even if they had made that supposition they could have no way of knowing which was which. The great fourteenth century zoologist Konrad von Mengenberg was able to doubt whether the dragon's breath is really fire (he suggests it may be just a poisonous humour), but he takes for granted that the animal really exists.[4]

Even in recent times, when this unquestioning faith began to fail, fear and superstition took its place and people still went on believing in the monster's real existence. Dragons were often seen in England and Wales as recently as the last century. Many sightings are recorded in the journal *Notes and Queries* and may easily be found by consulting the index under 'Dragon' (e.g. in the volumes for 1860-1880). The numerous British examples quoted by Simpson in 1980 reveal a strong belief in the reality of the animal up to recent times. John Ridgway claims to have encountered a sea-serpent when rowing across the Atlantic with Chay Blyth in 1965.[5] A well-known book on the dragon, published in 1928, was still able to say: "Millions of persons to-day have as firm a faith in its reality as in any fact, or supposed fact, of their intuition or experience" (Ingersoll, p.13).

Our ancestors not only knew the dragon and took his real existence for granted; they also feared him. A deep-rooted fear of the dragon is found in every part of the world, from the very earliest records of civilisation up to at least the nineteenth century. That fear was not irrational. As Freud distinguishes them, fear is a response to a real danger, while phobia is a response to an imagined one; and our modern animal fears are often phobias, like the sudden terror at night, when our nerves are not at their best, at the sight of a harmless mouse or a spider (which, up to the last century, was considered a lucky animal).[6] Similarly groundless is the fear inspired nowadays by the imaginary monsters of science fiction or horror films. But the primeval fear of dragons is different. It was the justifiable fear of a monster that quite certainly existed and was known to be exceptionally dangerous. The dragon may be for us a creature of the imagination, but he was real to those who feared him, and he has been feared by the overwhelming majority of human beings in all past ages.

The first and obvious problem about the dragon is its origin. How could it come about that ancient peoples everywhere came to believe in and to fear one specific animal which, in fact, had never·existed anywhere?

Some scholars have suggested that the common source of all dragons is a universal folk-memory of the enormous prehistoric reptiles which once walked this earth.[7] This we may cheerfully dismiss in view of the time

Fig. 1   *The Komodo Dragon.* From Carl Sagan, *The Dragons of Eden*, London: Hodder and Stoughton, 1977, where it appears by courtesy of the American Museum of Natural History.

scale. The last of the great saurians became extinct some sixty-five million years ago, long before the evolution of the first primates, let alone man.[8]

From those monsters a few fossil bones and still fewer fossil footprints have survived. These might perhaps, on the rare occasions when they were encountered, have helped to confirm early man's belief in great monsters. Simpson (p.16) mentions a dragon relief at Rentweisdorf near Coburg which appears to have been influenced by plesiosaur fossils of a type discovered in the slate mines of that area. At Klagenfurt (Carinthia) there is a fine 'dragon memorial', sculptured in 1590 by an artist who probably designed its head from the 'dragon's skull' found there in 1335, and now in the town's museum (Figure 2). The skull is actually that of a woolly rhinoceros from glacial times.[9] But such traces, which, beside their rarity, are usually so fragmentary as to mean little to anyone but the professional palaeontologist, can scarcely have been sufficient to create and form a picture of the whole animal in the imagination of our earliest ancestors.

It may seem more plausible that early man might have exaggerated the size of one or other of the small lizards that derive from those prehistoric reptiles, rather as science fiction today creates terrifying monsters by exaggerating the size of familiar small insects. But the lizards that survived till mankind appeared are different from the universal dragon: for example, they do not live in clouds or breathe anything like fire; few of them frequent water, and most avoid even damp situations. Nor do they have wings, although a few arboreal species, commonly known as 'flying dragons' (such as the Malay 'Draco volans') have a wing-like membraneous expansion which enables them to leap on to insects. Figure 3, of *Draco taeniopterus*, shows that these wing-like processes are not true wings, as they are quite independent of the fore limbs. Nor do they enable these small creatures (only about ten inches long, including the tail), to fly, but merely to make extensive leaps. Thus, even if we suppose that popular imagination exaggerates their size, and that this exaggeration happened similarly in every country, we still should have to explain how it came about that all races of mankind agreed in imagining an animal which is regularly different from the lizard.

There are also, as we have seen, some creatures of the sea which resemble the dragon, such as the great eels, giant squids and whales; these may sometimes be stranded on a beach and could thus have been encountered by early man. This might perhaps have given rise to the idea

Fig. 2   *The Klagenfurt 'Dragon Memorial'*. Photo from O. Abel, *Tiere der Vorzeit,* Berlin: Deutscher Verlag, 1939, p.82. (This is the supplementary fourth volume (Ergänzungsband) to Abel's *Das Reich der Tiere.*

The dragon features in many newspaper titles in Wales

of a sea-serpent. But these creatures, too, are clearly different from the dragon, which is universally a creature of the sky as well as the sea.

It seems that neither fossil traces nor any of the real beasts that live in this world can account for the origin of so distinct an animal as the dragon, though any of them may, at one time or another, have been mistaken for a dragon and in that way affected his local image and the way he was represented. Real animals may have influenced the dragon tradition, but they are not its beginning.

* * *

The dragon has sometimes been seen as one of the many fictitious beasts of the ancient Near East, a region rich in monsters and well placed for their transmission to both East and West.[10] To this region we owe, for example, the unicorn and the many races of weird wild men which, in the Middle Ages, were associated with India.

There is a broad consistency in the image, the habits and functions of dragons from China and India through Mesopotamia and the West which is difficult to account for except by diffusion from a common source. But such diffusion of beliefs about the dragon is more likely to have passed between peoples who already knew the monster and had strong feelings about him than into cultures that had never heard of him. We do not usually borrow cultural ideas from our neighbours unless we already have some interest in them and can apply the new ideas to our own existing knowledge and experience. The evident diffusion of ideas about the dragon suggests that people outside the Near East already knew him and feared him and therefore were interested in learning more about him.

The dragon pictures and beliefs found in pre-Columbian America, in Australasia and in the Pacific Islands show that some kind of indigenous dragon had been pre-existent in those cultures long before they became accessible to cultural diffusion from the Near East. Other fabulous beasts of the Near East were diffused to Europe through the authority of the ancient Greeks, from whom Europe derived so much of its science;[11] the dragon alone was already known in both East and West and did not come to Europe from the Greeks. Tales of the cosmic dragon, conquered by some god or hero, were circulating widely long before Greek times, and they featured largely in the myth and religion of all the early civilisations, from Egypt and Sumeria to China and Japan.

The dragon is also prominent in all cultural heraldry in the
Welsh tradition — the National Eisteddfod (above)
and the 'Urdd' — Welsh League of Youth (below)

Thus, the diffusion of dragon lore across Eurasia in the earliest times does not indicate one point of origin in the Near East. Instead, it favours the hypothesis that the dragon was already widely known when early societies began to exchange their stories about him and thus build up a reasonably consistent picture of his habits and appearance. It has been shown that early Germanic animal drawings were influenced by those of the Scythians, who themselves were in contact with the Chinese.[12] In this way diffusion may have created the large measure of agreement in the dragon traditions of widely separated cultures, while the basic idea of such an animal was everywhere pre-existent.

* * *

The original dragon was not copied directly either from nature or from neighbours. It was created everywhere in the minds of archaic peoples who felt a frightening awareness of some great and dangerous force, which must surely be animate, and which they needed to conceive in a definite, imaginable form. While we, since at least the time of the Greeks, have been inclined to personify the forces of nature (as with Father Time or the skeleton Death), our prehistoric forebears were more ready to conceive the great forces of nature in animal form, as may be seen in the oldest gods of India, China or Egypt (where the image of Death had the head of a jackal).

For our modern imagination the spirit of a particular season may be personified as Father Christmas, or the essence of a nation can be imagined as John Bull or Uncle Sam. In political debate especially we tend to identify a nation or a party with the person who leads it, because the person is easier for the mind to grasp, and for us to relate to, than any such amorphous abstraction as the concept of a nation or the policy of a political party. Similarly, our earliest ancestors had the need to grasp in some concrete form an image of the great but intangible forces that concerned them intensely and ruled their lives. But they did not have the modern view that animals are not persons. They could think of the dog, or the stag, the lion or the dragon in personal terms, as children still do today; they knew each animal's habits and qualities, his likes and dislikes, and they could use his image as a vehicle of their own hopes and fears.

Humans who were not yet convinced of human superiority over the animals had every reason to imagine the dominant forces of this world in animal rather than human form. They lived close to the animals, their

A 'gorsedd' of Llanrwst poets in the nineteenth century

own existence was equally precarious and they understood that their survival depended upon their living in harmony with nature. They could experience every day the superior powers of many animals and they had good reason to fear them. Knowing, for example, the sharpness of their senses and their uncanny awareness of the world around them (such as their ability to anticipate a change of weather, or the approach of an enemy), they attributed to animals still greater powers, such as that of predicting the future, and they assumed that animals and birds had their own form of language. Animals, like people, might be good or bad, lucky or unlucky, friendly or hostile, and it made sense for people to concentrate their fears upon the image of a frightening animal.

It has been well said that at the dawn of civilisation the predominant sensation of the more intelligent animals, and among them most especially man, must have been fear; and against the dreadful shapes and noises of the night, the shrieks of the gale, the thunder and lightning, the only defence known to man was humble propitiation and constant sacrifice.[13] In order to think of, to propitiate, indeed in any way to come to terms with the powers of destruction, the earliest human societies needed to give those powers an imaginable form.

The work of imagination was doubtless stimulated and much influenced by images of beasts already known and feared, above all by the images of snakes (such as the cosmic serpents of European and Asian mythology or the feathered and flying snakes of prehistoric Central and South America). Through the intercourse of peoples and their exchange of stories over thousands of years an increasingly consistent picture of the monster could be constructed, giving a clearer shape and more definite features to an idea that had begun as a vague but powerful sentiment, a strong sense of fear and awe which early man had needed to symbolise as a picture in the mind.

(ii) His Appearance and Nature

In his general appearance the prehistoric dragon resembles the snake more than any other animal (Figure 4). The snake always inspired great fear and respect, generally representing forces of chaos or evil; but sometimes he is a talisman (his poison is also a cure, and so he has become a symbol for medicine). Like the serpent, the dragon likes to bask in the sun, to lurk in trees, to swim in water, and his mouth is often so large that

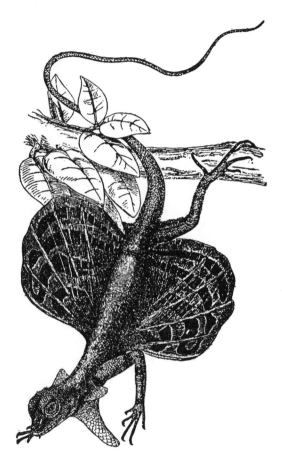

Fig. 3   *Draco taeniopterus*. From art. 'Dragon' in *Encyclopaedia Britannica*, 13th edition, 1926.

he can gobble up men and animals whole. In the East the dragon remains more snake-like than in the West.

The western dragon (Figure 5) is a product of our own Middle Ages. Old Europe, to the end of the Dark Ages, regularly shows its dragons in serpentine form, like those of the East. Even in Europe that image was never entirely supplanted by the squat, sometimes quadruped dragon of the Middle Ages. Naturally, the dragon's appearance varies in different times and places. He may vary in size, from large to fantastic; he may have two legs, or four, or none; he may be deaf and have no ears; he may or may not have horns: thousands of years and thousands of miles have understandably produced variations on the theme. Topsell, writing in the seventeenth century and following the final volume of Gesner's *Historia Animalium* of 1587, is well aware that foreign dragons are different from our own, and he described the varieties in some detail, recognising that the eastern dragon is longer and has a larger mouth.[14] A good description of the Chinese dragon is given by Wang Fu (during the Han Dynasty, 206B.C.—220A.D.) in his *Nine Resemblances*:[15]

> His horns resemble those of a stag, his head that of a camel, his eyes those of a demon, his neck that of a snake, his belly that of a clam, his scales those of a carp, his claws those of an eagle, his soles those of a tiger, his ears those of a cow.

One notices that there is no mention here of wings (Figure 6). Improbable as it may seem, Chinese dragon portraits do indeed generally conform to this pattern.

The dragon's most obvious difference from the serpent is that he is very much a creature of the air. He is universally associated with storms. In China torrential rain was called 'dragon rain';[16] in Middle Welsh *draig* ('dragon') was a common word for the lightning.[17] It was believed in East and West that storms were aroused when the dragon flew up into the clouds and disturbed the waters (and if two dragons should fight there would be a dreadful downpour). Consequently, in times of drought the rainmakers would use gongs to wake or frighten the dragon, so that he would fly up into the clouds. Confucius described the lofty thought of Lao Tsze in terms of this well-known habit of the dragon:[18]

> As to the dragon, we cannot understand his riding on the wind and his ascending to the sky. Today I saw Lao Tsze; is he not like the dragon?

The storm-raising dragon is also a creature of the water. Often his dwelling was assumed to be in marshy ground, if not directly in rivers or

Fig 4   *Ancestors of the Dragon.* From Ernest Ingersoll, *Dragons and Dragon Lore*, New York: Payson and Clarke, 1928, pp. 46-47.

lakes. The Japanese see the dragon as a river dweller: Allen and Griffiths say (p.41) that there is "some evidence that human sacrifices were made to river dragons." The same two authors note that, while the dragons of South America live in the sky, those of North America have generally lived in lakes (pp. 57ff). The Babylonian dragon Tiamat was a great sea-monster, not unlike the Old Testament Leviathan. The Anglo-Saxons remembered their hero Beowulf as the killer of a monstrous sea-dragon that lived in Grendel's lake. The old faith in large serpentine monsters that inhabit deep lakes is not altogether vanished today: the Highland Tourist Board cannot take all the credit for the traffic to Loch Ness (Figure 7). If a dragon in the clouds could raise storms, then a commotion of dragons in the water would cause floods. A dragon was seen in the Tiber at the great flood of Rome in 589, according to Gregory of Tours.[19] These watery associations of the dragon are also part of popular tradition in Wales, a place where rain, storms and floods have sometimes been known to occur.

The habitation of the dragon is always some lonely and desolate place, remote from the habitation of mankind. The prophet Job, being banished from human company, says (according to the Authorized Version or King James Bible) "I am a brother to dragons, and a companion to owls "(Job 30:29); similarly, when Babylon becomes a place of desolation "it shall be an habitation of dragons, and a court of owls" (Isaiah 34:13). (The Vulgate also has 'dragons' in these two contexts, but modern translations, including the Revised Version, replace this with 'jackals'). That view of his natural habitat is confirmed in every culture, from China and the Near East to Europe and the Americas. The dragon may live in the sky, or in the ocean or a great lake, or in some desolate, uninhabited place on the earth, but his home is always in the wilderness, the realm of primeval chaos, far away from civilisation and mankind. That is why he is seldom seen by man.

Being a creature of the air, as well as the water, the dragon has that keen eyesight which is otherwise associated with birds. In fact, the very word *dragon* (from Greek δρακων) is probably cognate with δερκειν, 'to see'. The keen eyesight of dragons is a feature stressed by Topsell in his encyclopaedia of 1658, where he assures his readers that, since we have so many reports of dragons, our knowledge of their characteristics is well founded.[20] The dragon's keen vision is known equally in the East, where an early Chinese text, the *Shan Hai King* (about the third century B.C.)

Fig.5 *The Western Squat Dragon*. After Gesner and Topsell, as in Jacqueline Simpson, *British Dragons*, London: Batsford, 1980, p.12.

says of the cosmic dragon: "with his looking he creates the daylight; by closing his eyes he makes the night".[21]

His keen-sightedness helps the dragon to perform his traditional function as the guardian of treasure. That point was made by Macrobius in the early fifth century: "dragons are assigned to be guardians of treasure because they are very keen of sight and remain awake at night".[22] Prosper Aquitanus, about the same time, reports that various sanctuaries, oracles, temples and treasures are guarded by dragons,[23] while Martial (late in the first century) had said of a miser that he guards his gold like a dragon.[24] In order to win the Golden Fleece, Jason must first kill the dragon that guards it; and Hercules likewise has to kill the dragon Ladon that guards the Golden Apples of the Hesperides. The Norse dragon Fafnir is also the guardian of a hoard of gold, as are the dragons which Beowulf slew; the burial mounds of the Anglo-Saxons, which contained treasure, were called 'hills of the dragon'. The Chinese, too, know the dragon as the guardian of hidden treasure and of precious minerals in the earth.[25] This is a universal feature and it is very old, though it appears more often in dragon stories of the West than in those of China and Japan.

★ ★ ★

The archaic dragon is a monster associated with powers of destruction. In creation myths he may represent the primeval chaos which is overcome by the gods who establish order. Thus, Zeus must overcome the primeval dragon Typhon: he buries it under Mount Etna, where it still occasionally shakes the earth and gives forth smoke.[26] An early Homeric hymn records how Apollo came to Delphi and killed there a great she-dragon (δράκαινα) which had attacked and killed all who passed that way: that report is an archaic form of the legend of Apollo's great victory over the dragon Python.[27] Myths of the Hittites record the combat between the Weather God and the dragon Illuyankas.[28] In Egypt both Osiris, originally a fertility god, and Ra, the sun god, must overcome a dragon representing chaos and destruction, while the god Seth is represented as destroying each morning the sun-eating dragon Apophis, so that night may pass and a new day begin (Figure 8).

In Norse mythology the Tree of the World, Yggdrasil, has its roots perpetually gnawed by the serpent Nidhoggr, while the dragon Fafnir is overcome on behalf of humanity by Sigurdr. According to Snorri's *Edda*, the god Thor, at the end of the world, will fish for the cosmic snake that

28

Fig.6   *Chinese Serpentine Dragon*. From Ralph Whitlock, *Here be Dragons*, London: Allen and Unwin, 1983, p.36.

embraces the world (*midgardsormr*) and catch him. The Hindu god Indra overcomes the dragon Vrthra (i.e. 'the Writher'); the Babylonian god Marduk conquers the sea-dragon Tiamat[29] (Figure 9). Such divine victories as these are celebrated in festivals, which also strengthen the image of the dragon as a great enemy who represents primeval chaos which has been overcome by the god. For that reason the dragon is readily associated with evil.

It may be, however, that those untamed and chaotic natural forces which the god has conquered are not in themselves evil, but simply the given condition of nature. The many early representations that show a dragon swallowing the sun certainly make him appear ominous; but he is also often shown regurgitating the sun (hence he is responsible for eclipses), and that process may be understood as a necessary part of the rhythm of nature. The Norse dragon Fafnir (i.e. 'the Encircler') not only encircles and threatens the earth, he also holds it together. In Mexico the feathered serpent Quetzalcoatl (from *quetzal*, 'bird', and *coatl*, 'water-serpent') is a primeval monster demanding human sacrifice, yet also the giver of rain and fertility and a symbol of life and resurrection.[30] Thus, though the prehistoric dragons of mythology threaten civilisation, it seems they were also a necessary part of the cosmic process. They were therefore not conceived as wholly evil beings.

It is in the traditions of the West that the dragon becomes wholly and conspicuously evil. The dragon has a thoroughly bad image already in the Old Testament: it has been argued that the priests of Jehovah (themselves possibly heirs of a moon-cult had to compete with dragon-cults in establishing the priority of their religion and for that reason they saw the dragon as wholly evil.[31] The prophets foretell that the dragon shall be destroyed (Psalm 91:13, AV; Isaiah 27:1) and the psalmist envisages for him a still greater humiliation, when the dragon shall be called upon to praise Jehovah (Psalm 148:7). It may be that the serpent of Eden, which seems to guard the Tree of Knowledge, had been a dragon until it was cursed by Jehovah to go on its belly and eat dust: that curse would have had little force if the beast concerned had already been a serpent without legs or wings.[32]

The early Christians made the monstrous dragon into a figure of Satan (Revelation 12:3, 12:9 and thereafter the mediaeval bestiaries); the fruit of that idea may be seen on the cathedral door at Hildesheim, where a bronze relief (dated about 1008-1015) shows a dragon whispering into the ear of Pilate at the trial of Jesus.[33] Christian saints and folk-heroes are forever

Fig. 7   *Highland Tourist Board Cartoon:* From 'A Selection of Cartoons' by Jak from the London Evening Standard Book Number 3 (Sept. 13, 1969). Beaverbrook Newspapers Ltd., London, 1970.

    Seth Spearing Apophis. From Francis Huxley, *The Dragon*, London: Thames and Hudson, 1979, p.78. Seth, sailing in the sun-boat of Horus over the waters where Apophis, dragon of chaos, lives, kills the monster so that a new day may come.

despatching dragons, and their moral rectitude is unquestioned: there is no such thing as a good dragon or a bad saint. This view of the dragon was favoured by the moralistic and monotheistic nature of the religion. Where there is only one god and he is the source of all goodness, his antagonist must be wholly evil: God's imposition of order upon chaos was more than a fact of history or a process of nature, it was also the triumph of good over evil. While the primeval dragon of prehistory had been threatening, the dragon now became wicked. But this wickedness was not, like his ferocity, a universal feature. It applied only in the Christian West, and there it prevented the development of the revered, benevolent dragon which is celebrated today at popular festivals in the East.

Except, of course, in Wales.

(iii) The Cult of the Dragon

Everywhere the dragon was feared; and fear is close to respect. Thus it is that cults may arise which celebrate the very beings which a society most fears. Millions of Hindus worship the most dreadful aspect of the destroyer-god Shiva in the form of the black goddess Kali, who drinks human blood and often wears a garland of human skulls: to her the city of Calcutta (*Kali-gat*) is dedicated. Among the Vikings the fickle and bloodthirsty Odin, who never tires of stirring up quarrels so that he may drive good men to their deaths, became the greatest of gods. Often it is the god of thunder who earned the respect and worship of ancient peoples. The dreaded Furies, from whom the Greeks expected nothing but death, were called by them εὐμενίδες, 'the well-meaning ones' and Greek sailors, who feared to cross the Black Sea, called it εὔξεινος, 'kind to strangers'. In many ancient societies, including that of Egypt, the poisonous snake became an object of reverence, even of kingship. So also with the dragon: ancient peoples responded to the animal not only with fear, but also with respect, and by propitiating the monster they might even hope to win its friendship and protection.

The religion of the ancient Babylonians is centred on the conquest of a dragon; yet dragons, together with bulls, guard the Ishtar gate at Babylon, 700-600 B.C. Hercules is famous as a dragon-killer; yet, according to Hesiod's *The Shield of Hercules*, he bore the image of a dragon upon his shield. The article 'Serpent-Worship' in the *Encyclopaedia Britannica* (13th edn., 1926) tells of kings and heroes supposedly fathered by a dragon. Germanic warriors carried dragon-ornamented swords and lances which, like the dragon's tongue, might be poisoned, and there was a

32

Fig.9   *Marduk in Combat With a Dragon*. From a cylinder seal in the
             British Museum reproduced by J. Fontenrose, *Python*,
             Berkeley/Los Angeles: University of California Press, 1959,
             facing p.148. Also reproduced in Simpson (as cited for Fig.5
             above), facing p.64, and called there 'Babylonian cylinder
             seal. The god Marduk, wielding thunderbolts, triumphs
             over the dragon Tiamat'.

Fig. 10   *Serpents and Dragons on Celtic Coins from the Second Century
             B.C.* from Jan Filip, *Celtic Civilization and its Heritage*,
             second, revised edition, Wellingborough: Collet's, and
             Prague: Academia, 1977, pp. 136, 140.

dragon cult associated with the war-god Odin.[34] The Viking longship was commonly called *dreki* ('dragon') and it had a dragon's head carved at the prow. A thousand or more years before the Viking *dreki*, the first Phoenician ships entered the Persian gulf, with — so Ingersoll, p.44, notes — animal or bird heads and two big eyes on the bows. Sometimes the Vikings would remove or cover the dragon's head as they approached land, for fear of offending the gods or spirits of the place. Thus the law of Ulfljót (c. 930 A.D.) required the dragon prow to be removed lest it frighten the *land vaettir* (spirits of the land). But at sea the Vikings needed the dragon's protection and so they kept his head in front. Similarly, the ridge-beams of early Germanic houses often ended in a carved dragon. These people evidently recognised that the dragon was a ferocious and dangerous beast, and precisely for that reason they sought to engage him as their protector.

Erasmus once observed that the device chosen by wise men to represent kings is the eagle, which is cruel and murderous, not musical or beautiful, and confers no benefit on mankind. He considered the choice appropriate.[35] Similarly whole nations, since the earliest times, have preferred to take the deadliest of beasts as their emblems: the Vulture and the Cobra were chosen to be the sacred animals of Lower and Upper Egypt (where the crocodile also was worshipped). In north east India and Tibet, the man-eating tiger, as well as the dragon, was venerated.[36] The English chose the lion. Precisely because of the dread which such animals inspired they were suitable candidates to be propitiated by sacrifice, venerated in cult and totem, and proudly chosen as the emblem for a people or a king. And chief among the dreaded beasts was the dragon.

Gesner and Topsell describe the dragon as the king of the serpents, following a tradition that goes back to Isidore, the sixth century Archbishop of Seville.[37] Just as the lion is the king of the animals and the eagle king of the birds, so, for feudal Europe is the dragon the king of serpents. This view of his pre-eminence among his kind accords with the special interest shown in the dragon in East and West and it makes him a suitable emblem of kingship. The Emperors of Byzantium adopted the dragon as the sign of their authority; thus Artemidorus explains: "On account of its strength the Dragon signifies the Emperor and senior official".[38] And so the dragon standard was used by the Byzantine Emperors in ceremonial and in battle.

In China the dragon is famous as the sign of the Emperor, and imperial soldiers fought under the dragon flag. The imperial throne was called the

ETSYRIAM SOBAL· ET CONVERTIT
IOAB· ET PERCUSSIT EDOMINVAL
LESALINARVM·XII MILIA·

Fig. 11   *Horsemen with Dragon Standard.* From the Psalterium
Aureum or Golden Psalter of the late ninth century, St.
Gallen, Stiftsbibliothek. Reproduced as Plate XI in J. Rudolf
Rahn, *Das Psalterium Aureum von St. Gallen,* St. Gallen,
1878. The picture depicts the army of Joab setting out to do
battle with the Syrians and with the Ammonites (2 Samuel
10:9ff; 1 Chronicles 19:10). Rahn thinks that the ninth
century artist drew the picture from personal experience of
such processions: the Emperor and other high dignitaries
had visited the monastery at St. Gallen repeatedly (pp. 33, 42
n.86).

Fig. 12   *St. George Fighting Dragon*. Fifteenth-century wall-painting, St. Gregory's Church, Norwich; from Simpson (as cited for Fig. 5 above), between pp. 64 and 65.

'dragon's seat', the princes were the 'dragon's seed'; and when the Emperor died, they said "the Dragon has risen". The artist working on a wall in the Imperial palace at Peking failed to include one of the requisite number of dragons, and this was interpreted as a bad omen for the Manchu dynasty.[39] The Emperor himself was called *T'ien Lung*, 'Celestial Dragon'. But the Chinese dragon is not only the sign of the Emperor: he is also a king in his own right, known as *Lung Wang*, the Dragon King. The Dragon King bestows blessings, particularly rain and fertility, and he is generally benevolent, though he can be nasty when crossed.[40] His birthday is a national holiday, marked by festive ceremonies involving dragon processions. Thus, in China the dragon became both a royal and a popular national symbol.

Such a development would seem impossible in the West, where the dragon became a symbol of all that is evil and where we celebrate not the dragon, but the dragon killer in our popular traditions. And yet in Wales the dragon became as popular as he is in China. Though in Wales he is not specifically an emblem of kingship, nor associated with any particular Welsh family, the dragon stands for the identity of the nation and he has represented national independence for as long as the nation has existed.

The Welsh, as a distinct people, may be said to date from about the seventh century, when the advance of the Saxons to the Bristol Channel and the Mersey isolated them from the rest of Celtic Britain. The *Historia Brittonum*, of about 800 A.D. (traditionally ascribed to the scholar Nennius),[41] which drew on earlier sources, described a Red Dragon as the symbol of the British people in their wars against the White Dragon of the Saxons. This relates to a time when the Welsh, as a people distinct from other Britons, did not yet exist. Early in the Welsh literary tradition, in the tale *Lludd a Llefelys*, this Red Dragon is associated with Merlin, who gives counsel to the earliest kings of Britons.[42] Thus, the Red Dragon, which is still very prominent in Welsh life today, has accompanied the Welsh people from the very beginning of their history.

When Harri Tudur from Wales fought for the title Henry VII
on Bosworth field, he did so flying the red dragon
at the head of his Welsh army.

Chapter 2

The Dragon of Britain

(i) Introduction

The island of Britain, like all the rest of the world, has been haunted by dragons since prehistoric times. The earliest known artifacts of the Celts, while not clearly showing the dragon, do give very clear evidence of a lively serpent-cult, and it is sometimes unclear whether the serpent is an ordinary snake or a dragon.[1] Prehistoric Celtic pictures (mostly on torcs) of about 500 B.C. show a god (evidently Cernunnos) together with a horned snake around his neck or his waist.[2] Brooches and pins bearing serpent images were worn during the La Tène period (the final five centuries B.C.),[3] and *fibulae* (enamelled brooches) bearing dragons were worn by Britons during the Roman occupation.[4] Celtic scabbards decorated with pairs of dragons, dating from the period around 300 B.C., have been found throughout the Celtic world, from central Europe to London.[5] Serpents, some of them possibly dragons, appear on Celtic coins from the second century B.C. (see Figure 10). The serpent or snake was important in the religion of the Druids.[6] Some of their high priests were known by the name *gwiberod*, 'vipers',[7] and they held in great reverence the *maen magl* or *glain neidr*, the 'serpent stone', a ball of amber thought to be made by snakes and used until recently in healing eye complaints.[8] It has been suggested that the serpents which St. Patrick banished from Ireland may have been emblems of pagan Celtic gods and protectors of pagan warriors.[9] Evidently the earliest Celts not only feared but also venerated the serpent, and, while the evidence is inadequate for proof, it is likely that the king of serpents, the dragon, whose image Celts wore during the Roman period, had been an object of fear and veneration among them before the Romans arrived.

With the advent of a written literature, the Celts come out into the clearer light of history, and then the importance of dragons in their culture becomes very obvious. The tale of *Lludd a Llefelys*, written down about 1200 but based on ancient material, preserves a tale of two monstrous dragons destroyed at Oxford long ago by King Lludd, who overcomes them by a trick (he fills a pit with mead, with which they intoxicate themselves). The *Peredur* tale tells of a dragon that keeps a gold ring and another that sits on a treasure mound; the hero kills them both. A number of dragon-killings are recorded also by Geoffrey of Monmouth, and future ones are among the prophecies of Merlin.[10] Several Welsh saints are remembered as dragon killers, most famously St. Patrick, who killed all the serpents of Ireland (his name, *Padraig,* was interpreted by popular etymology as *pa draig* 'what dragon?'); but also St. Samson, who tied a girdle round the neck of a great dragon and cast it into the sea.[11] There are similar tales of St. Llwchaearn.[12]

The Welsh, like other cultures, associate the dragon with the clouds and the lightning: the Welsh word *draig* is attested from the fourteenth and fifteenth centuries as meaning 'sheet-lightning'.[13] In many Welsh tales the dragon is represented as flying in the clouds.[14] Welsh folklore is packed with stories of loathsome dragons, and these persisted into recent times.[15] The fiery dragon of the thunder-clouds, the hostile and dangerous monster that threatens harmless people, together with the popular hero who overcomes the dragon, are all well known in Wales. But, as everybody knows, the dragon in Wales is more than all that: the Welsh dragon is a military and a national emblem and he stands for the spirit and the national independence of the Welsh people.

(ii) The Military Dragon of Rome

The dragon as a military standard was brought to Britain by the Romans who had encountered the dragon used as a battle flag by the Scythians, Indians, Persians, Parthians and Dacians. Among the Indians and Parthians a unit of 1,000 men was regularly assembled under the dragon flag.[16] Trajan's Column, erected at Rome in 113 A.D., shows a dragon standard being borne aloft by Dacian soldiers, another flying dragon in front of a Dacian position, and some more partially concealed dragon emblems among the trophies of victory taken by the Romans.[17] The Romans themselves adopted the dragon about 175 A.D. and were using it as the standard for the cohort by the third century. From this time on, while the legions had their traditional Eagle, the cohort had the Dragon. The bearer of the cohort's standard was called the *draconarius*; he carried a gilded staff with the dragon at its top. Either the Dacian or the Parthian battle dragon is likely to be the source of this Roman military dragon.[18]

Vegetius, writing at the end of the fourth century, repeatedly mentions the dragon as the battle sign of the cohort, borne by the *draconarius*:[19]

Primum signum totius legionis est aquila, quam aquilifer portat. Dracones etiam per singulas cohortes a draconariis feruntur ad proelium.

(The first emblem of the whole legion is the Eagle, which is carried by the aquilifer. The dragons, however, are borne into battle by the draconarii of the individual cohorts).

Tatlock (p.224) gives evidence that the dragon emblem was retained in Constantinople as an army ensign and also, among other banners, carried before the emperor by great officials on certain occasions. Ammianus Marcellinus records that the Emperor Constantius II, arriving in Rome in military attire like a triumphator, "was surrounded by dragons, woven out of purple thread and bound to the golden and jewelled tops of spears, with wide mouths open to the breeze and hence hissing as if roused by anger, and leaving their tails winding in the wind." Reporting on the imperial dragon, as used in battle in the east in 357 A.D., Ammianus says that the emperor's cavalry recognised him "by the purple ensign of a dragon, fitted to the top of a very long lance and spreading out like the slough of a serpent".[20] Gesner, in the final volume of his *Historia Animalium* (1587), quotes the poet Claudian's reference to Constantius' entry into Rome: "mansuescunt varii vento cessante dracones" — rendered by Topsell, in his adaptation of Gesner's book, as: "When whistling winde in air ceast/The Dragons tamed then did rest".[21] In the Roman west, a similar wind-inflated battle-dragon is described by Sidonius, writing in 458 in praise of the Emperor Maiorianus, who had done battle with Vandal invaders a few months before:[22]

iam textilis anguis

discurrit per utramque aciem, cui guttur adactis
turgescit zephyris; patulo mentitur hiatu
iratam pictura famen, pannoque furorem
aura facit quotiens crassatur vertile tergum
flatibus et nimium iam non capit alvus inane.

(Now the broidered dragon speeds hither and thither in both armies, his throat swelling as the zephyrs dash against it; that pictured form with wide-open jaw counterfeits a wrathful hunger, and the breeze puts a frenzy into the cloth as often as the lithe back is thickened by the blasts and the air is now too abundant for the belly to hold.)

Here, too, the Dragon is the sign not merely of a cohort, but of the Roman Emperor himself, this time at war with barbarians, and, as in the context of Ammianus, the military dragon flies above the army, billowing and thrashing about in the air and hissing like the dreaded beast itself.

This flying monster was likely not only to frighten the enemy, for whom the dragon of nature was real enough, but also to impress the ordinary soldiery of the Roman army, drawn together by this time from many barbarian provinces. The fear which the flying dragon standard inspired among the superstitious soldiery of Rome and her enemies, and continued to inspire in the soldiers of mediaeval Europe, is expressly mentioned in many of the passages which refer to the dragon, as Tatlock has pointed out.[23] Typical are the lines in the twelfth century romance of *Athis et Prophilias:*[24]

> *Ce souloient Romains porter,*
> *Ce nous fait moult à redouter.*
>
> (This the Romans used to carry; this makes us very much to be feared)

This artificial beast is clearly the source of the word for 'kite' in a number of European languages (e.g. German *Drache*, Scandinavian and Old English *drake*).

With their use of the billowing dragon of the battlefield throughout the Middle Ages, the peoples of Europe continued to recognise that the dragon's place is in the clouds. And whilst the δρακοντεῖον, or dragon banner, became especially important for ceremonial in the eastern part of the Empire, its univeral use as the standard of the cohort, its use as a battle flag in the third century, and the lasting impression it made on the military practice of western as well as eastern Europe, show that this dragon was firmly established as a battle standard thoughout the Roman world long before the Empire was divided into separate eastern and western parts (Figure 11).

In the last centuries of the Roman occupation of Britain the military Dragon must have been seen much more often than the Eagle. That is not simply because cohorts were ten times more numerous than legions, but also because, as the imperial grip on Britain faltered and troop numbers declined (soldiers being withdrawn to the continent and not replaced), the army in Britain generally operated on the basis of the cohort.[25] The nature of the problem, which consisted of a large number of small-scale incursions, made prompt local action by a cohort more effective than the slow mobilisation of legions. Thus, those people who were left behind when the legions withdrew forever must most naturally have thought of the Dragon as the symbol of that Roman civilisation to which they belonged and which they were now defending against the ravages of barbarian invaders. It is generally agreed that resistance to the Saxons was first organised by Romans, or Romanised Britons, presumably on Roman lines; such men had Roman names, like Ambrosius Aurelianus and, no doubt, Artorius (Arthur). For their battle standard no emblem was more natural than the familiar Dragon of the Roman cohort.

(iii) The Old Welsh Military Dragon

The period after the Roman departure is not well documented; nevertheless, there are sufficient references to the dragon for us to be sure that he continued to play a significant part in the life of the people. From the very first records of the Welsh language the words *draig, dragon* mean 'warrior' and great warriors are referred to as *pendraig, pendragon*, i.e. 'chief dragon'.

It is possible that this usage has nothing to do with the military dragon of the Romans, since the very nature of the dragon makes an association with the warrior probable. In the oldest of the Greek dragon legends, Cadmus, founder of Thebes, slays the dragon of the place and plants its teeth into the ground, and from that spot grow armed warriors. Such modern words as 'dragoon' show how the word can come to refer to a soldier. It might happen anywhere. But the late Roman military use of the dragon standard, though not demonstrably its source, can only have strengthened the association of the dragon with the warrior in Britain.[26]

Gildas, writing about 540 A.D., refers to the British chieftain Maglocunus (known to the Welsh as Maelgwn Gwynedd) as "insularis draco".[27] This use of 'dragon' may or may not be significant, since Gildas applies the names of other animals to leading warriors ('the Lion', 'the Panther', 'the Bear'). A successor of Maglocunus to the lordship of Anglesey, Gruffudd ap Llywelyn, is described as "draic o wyned" ('Dragon of Gwynedd') in a poem of the eleventh century preserved in the late fourteenth century *Red Book of Hergest*; but by this time the use of 'dragon' for an army leader was well established.

We are on firmer ground when we look at the first records of the Welsh language and find there that warriors are commonly referred to as dragons. Thanks to the researches of Sir Ifor Williams we know that the main part of Aneirin's *Gododdin*, together with certain of the heroic

43

poems attributed to Taliesin, though not written down until centuries later, may well represent in fact the language and culture of the late sixth century A.D.[28] Since bardic traditions were conservative, these texts give a good record of their period of composition. The background to these earliest Welsh poems is not yet Wales, but northern England and southern Scotland, and the people are still called *Brythoniaid*, 'Britons'; the term *Cymry*, 'Welsh', begins to appear only from the middle of the seventh century, when the people of that region were becoming conscious of their separate identity. This poetry thus carries us back to a time before the Welsh nation existed, when the Welsh people were only beginning to emerge out of the Britons who had been driven to the west and north of the island.

Already in this literature the terms *dreic, dragon* abound. The *Gododdin* mentions the 'feast of the dragon', meaning the feast of Mynyddog.[29] Since Mynyddog Mwynfawr was the patron of the poet, Aneirin, it is clear that the term 'dragon' is meant to be complimentary. Aneirin refers to Gwernabwy mab Gwën as a dragon at the battle of Catraeth.[30] An early Taliesin poem on Urien of Rheged distinguished the *dreic dylaw* ('inexperienced dragon', i.e. bad leader) from the *dreic hylaw* ('skilful dragon'). Owain ap Urien is called *Owain ben draic*, the 'chief dragon'. In a poem on Gwallawc, Taliesin begins with an army lamenting the fall of their 'dragon':[31]

> En enw gwledic nef gorchordyon. rychanant
> rychwynant y dragon.
>
> (In the name of the Lord the armies sing out and lament their dragon)

In the individual case quotations like these prove nothing, since a line may be corrupt or may be a late interpolation. But the use of *draig* for 'warrior' or 'leader' is so frequent as to establish general usage: it is entirely characteristic of the earliest known Welsh poetry, and it remains standard in both Old and Middle Welsh, through the whole of the Middle Ages. it is, of course, amply recorded in the standard dictionaries. Thus, in *GPC*:

> *dragon*: warrior, hero, war-leader, chieftain, prince, military power.
> *dragonol*: ferocious, brave, valiant, warrior, brave fighter.
> *dragonwys*: draconic, ferocious, brave.
> *dragwn*: dragon, warrior, hero, war-leader, chieftain.

44

draig:
1. dragon
2. warrior, hero, war-leader, chieftain, prince
3. Satan, the Devil
4. sheet-lightning, lightning unaccompanied by thunder, meteorite

Similarly, D. Silvan Evans in his *Geiriadur Cymraeg*:

dragon, dragwn:
1(a) a dragon
  (b) the dragon (as an emblem or symbol)
2 — a leader (in war), a commander, a chief.

dragonawl: leading, commanding, foremost, supreme, heroic.
dragoni: to act as leader, to command (an army etc).
dragonwys: leaders, commanders, heroes.
dragwn: dragon.
draig:
1. a dragon.
2. the dragon (as a symbol, or a military standard etc.; also figuratively).
3. the dragon, applied metaphorically to "the old Serpent, called the Devil, and Satan".
4. a leader, commander, ruler, or chief; a hero.
5. the constellation Dragon (Draco).

Both of these dictionaries give ample examples, going back to Aneirin and Taliesin.

Together with the genuine Taliesin poems, which give us our most archaic record of the Welsh language, we have many prophetic verses attributed to Taliesin, foretelling the coming liberation from the Saxon yoke. These poems cannot be so very early, since most of them promise the return of Cadwaladr (who died in 664),[32] but they are likely to be not much later than the seventh century and nearly all of them belong clearly to the pre-Norman period. Thus, while the Danes are often mentioned, only one of these poems suggests any knowledge of the Normans.[33] Here too, the word 'dragon' described the warrior chief and, together with other compliments ('the bear', 'the lion') it refers to the coming deliverer, who is called *draig ffawd ffyst gychwyned*, 'the fated Dragon, quick to rise'.

(iv) **The Red Dragon and Saxon Dragons**

By the time the *Historia Brittonum* was written, about 800 A.D. following chronicles of an earlier period, the dragon is not only the individual soldier, and not the coming deliverer, but a symbol of national independence, and, for the first time, the national dragon is described as red. Although, as we saw (above p.37 and note), the ascription of this compilation to the scholar Nennius is merely traditional, to avoid circumlocution I shall call its author by this name. He records a story which can be paraphrased as follows:

> King Vortigern determines to build a fortress in Snowdonia, but while his workmen gather together the timber and stones during the day, these materials regularly disappear mysteriously during the night. Vortigern summons his magicians, who tell him that he must first find a child that has no father, kill him and sprinkle the place with his blood.
>
> Such a boy is found, and the King tells him why he is to be killed. The boy bids the King summon his magicians and tells them there is a pool beneath the place. They dig and find the pool, and then the boy shows them that there are vessels in the pool, and a piece of cloth between them, and in the cloth are two serpents, a red one and a white one. The white serpent drives the red one back almost to the edge of the cloth, but then the red one recovers and drives the white serpent off the cloth and away across the pool.
>
> Asked what this signifies, the boy explains that these are two dragons. The red dragon is the dragon of the British people, and the white dragon represents that nation that has seized so much of Britain and will hold the land, almost from sea to sea; but then the Britons will arise and drive the usurpers off across the sea. The boy reveals that his name is Ambrosius and his father is a Roman consul (or emperor).

This story shows the Red Dragon perfectly clearly as the emblem of the Welsh nation. The Roman origin of Ambrosius (whose fortress stands at Dinas Emrys — Emrys being the Welsh name for Ambrosius — near Beddgelert) suggests a Roman origin for his dragon. If the father of Ambrosius is indeed to be understood as a Roman emperor, then there may be a connection with the imperial red dragon of the eastern Roman

Empire; in any event it is clear that the context of the dragon is military — agreeing entirely with the earliest use of the word *draig, dragon* — and that the Red Dragon was, at some date earlier than 800 A.D., understood as the military symbol of British resistance. Its essential meaning has scarcely changed from that day to this.

Thus Nennius establishes the Red Dragon of Wales at some date earlier than 800 A.D. But we also have a much older text which appears to allude to the same story. The *gorchan* of Maeldderw, in the *Book of Aneirin*, which is an elegiac lay believed to be by Aneirin and contemporary with the *Gododdin*, about 600 A.D., contains a mysterious passage:

> Disgleiryawr ac archawr taḷ achon
> arrud dhreic fud pharaon (11.1431-2, p.56 of Sir Ifor Williams'
> edition of *Canu Aneirin*)

It is difficult to make any sense of this, or indeed of the whole poem, the transmission of which appears to be corrupt. But the words *rud dhreic* must surely mean 'red dragon', and *pharaon* occurs also in the prose tale *Lludd a Llefelys*, which also records the story of the two dragons on Snowdon. According to the tale, 'Dinas Ffaraon Dandde' was the old name of the fortress near Beddgelert which later became known as 'Dinas Emrys'. This name occurs also in *Trioedd Ynys Prydein* (number 13).[34] Thus, while the text is admittedly too corrupt to carry a great theory, it does appear to refer to the Red Dragon of Nennius: and since we have no cause to doubt either the authenticity of the line or the early date of the *gorchan* of Maeldderw, it seems that the tale of the national Red Dragon of the Britons was current as early as 600 A.D., some two centuries before it was written down in Latin by Nennius.

The legend recorded by Nennius, and known in other, more elaborate versions from the twelfth century onwards,[35] bears witness not only to the Red Dragon of Wales: it mentions also another dragon, which is white and associated with the Saxons. Dragon traditions were just as strong among the Germanic tribes as among the Celts, and the Saxons, both in Britain and on the continent, made use of dragon standards in battle. There is a tradition that Cuthred, King of Wessex, used a dragon standard when he defeated the Mercians at Burford in 752, and that Edmund Ironside bore the dragon against King Canute in 1016.[36] The Saxon historian Widukind of Corvey, writing in the tenth century, mentions the dragon among battle signs sacred to the Saxons.[37] The Bayeux Tapestry shows King Harold falling at Hastings beside a dragon standard. Such use of the dragon among the Saxons led Tatlock to conclude that the Welsh dragon itself was derived from this Saxon battle-dragon. He argued his case in his important article of 1933, to which I have repeatedly referred, and which has decisively influenced opinion concerning the origin of the Welsh dragon.

There is no doubt about the importance of the dragon among the Germanic peoples. We find dragons on ships, roof-beams and ridges, and frequently on Germanic armour. The Sutton Hoo shield (c. 650 A.D.) is liberally adorned with dragons. In this the traditions of Germanic people scarcely differ from those of the Celts. But Tatlock's examples of its use as a battle standard among the Saxons of Britain are not so compelling. Of the three examples he quotes (Cuthred, Edmund and Harold), the first two are taken from the chronicle of Henry of Huntingdon, who is not a very reliable source and who wrote in the twelfth century, when the dragons of Arthur were well known to the Normans and might easily be attributed by a Norman writer to earlier British kings. The sentence from Widukind mentions the dragon only as one among several emblems represented on the sacred standard and does not imply any special importance for the dragon. Only the Bayeux Tapestry seems to show a clear Saxon dragon standard, and that, in view of the linguistic and literary evidence, is too late to constitute a possible origin for the dragon of Wales.

The greatest weakness in Tatlock's case is his dating of the native Welsh material, which includes references to the military and national dragons of the Britons. He puts the poems of Aneirin and Taliesin only a little earlier than their manuscripts, which date from the thirteenth and fourteenth centuries. For this we must not blame him; we today have the benefit of hindsight, which is the clearest form of vision. Tatlock was writing a few years before the researches of Sir Ifor Williams established beyond reasonable doubt a very much earlier dating of much of the material in these documents. It was in 1938 that Sir Ifor published his now famous edition of the *Gododdin*, which showed that the poem and its *gorchanau* were composed in the north about 600, and in subsequent studies Sir Ifor identified the genuine verses of Taliesin, also dating from about 600, from within the larger corpus of writings handed down under that name.[38] The conclusions of Sir Ifor about the dating of these works gained rapid acceptance and were confirmed again more recently by Kenneth Jackson.[39] It is agreed that the texts may have been corrupted during the centuries of oral transmission; but their language is genuinely archaic and in those texts the use of *draig, dragon* for 'war-leader' is not isolated, but entirely normal, not in one particular text, but in the generality of Welsh texts from the earliest records of the language. That usage may be traced from the period about 600 up to the threshold of modern times.

As long as the Welsh literary material was thought to begin in the thirteenth century, or only a little earlier, then it was reasonable to argue that there was no early evidence of the military dragon in Wales apart from Nennius. But since we can now reliably go back to a period some two centuries earlier than him, his testimony is no longer isolated. We now know that the dragon was a common term for the warrior, and so it is perfectly intelligible that two dragons in conflict should signify the warring peoples of Wales and England, as Nennius says. Since 'dragon' for 'soldier' was common usage by 600, and the Red Dragon attested as emblem of the nation by 800, it becomes much more likely that the Welsh derived the Red Dragon from their own traditions, which in turn recalled the Roman cohort standard under which they had fought for their civilisation against the Saxon invaders, rather than that they copied it from the Saxon enemy.

The only thing that remains unclear about the early British dragon is its colour. According to Nennius, the dragon of the Britons is red. We have seen that the phrase 'red dragon' occurs as early as Aneirin, though in a passage of dubious meaning. We know that the Roman dragon of the eastern Empire was red; but we have no clear connection between that Roman dragon and the national British dragon which Nennius records. The national dragon of mediaeval Wales may be red, or fiery, or golden. Thus the evidence that the dragon of Wales was red from the earliest times is inconclusive. It may be that his colour was not yet fixed, though he was thought to resemble fire, his most natural element: for the colours, on those occasions when colour is mentioned, are those appropriate to fire, and never any other. It may be regarded as a general rule that the colours of flags were not fixed before about the twelfth century. What mattered was the emblem, not its colour: rather than *represent* something, the banner *was* something. Up to the twelfth century the banner of the Holy Roman Empire, for instance, might be gold, red and gold, or silver and gold.[40]

(v) The Dragon of Arthur

According to Geoffrey of Monmouth, writing about 1136, that most famous king of the Britons, King Arthur, bore a dragon as his emblem. In Geoffrey's *Historia Regum Britanniae* Arthur appears in battle with a golden dragon standard ("aureum draconem infixit quem pro vexillo habebat"), and his helmet also bears the dragon emblem ("aurem galeam simulachro draconis insculptam capiti adaptat"). He dreams of a fiery dragon, who flies in from the west and lights up the land with the brightness of his eyes, and those around him are quick to recognise that the dragon is Arthur himself.[41] The many poets who follow Geoffrey's

History are quick to transmit the idea of the dragon as the emblem of Arthur; thus Robert Wace wrote, in his *Roman de Brut*, about the year 1155:[42]

> ensom ot portrait un dragon

Similarly, Robert of Gloucester says:[43]

> Wyth helm of gold on ys heued, (nas nour hym ylych)
> The fourme of a dragon thereon was ycast.

And in a Welsh version of Geoffrey's *Historia Regum*, we read of Arthur's 'golden dragon' (dreic eureit) — his standard:[44]

> A rac bron Arthur sefyll y dreic eureit yr honn a oed yn lle arwyd idaw.

Geoffrey also attributes to Arthur a father named Uther Pendragon, and he understands the epithet as meaning 'dragon's head' ("vocatus fuit Uther Pendragon, quod Britannica lingua capud drachonis sonamus").[45] Here too, the poets who follow Geoffrey accept both the tradition and the interpretation of the epithet 'Pendragon', which becomes an emblem and a heraldic device for Uther. Layamon calls him:[46]

> Pendragun an Brutisc, Draken-hefd an Englisc
> (Pendragon in British, Dragon's-head in English)

And in *Perlesvaus* he figures as "roi Uter Pandragon".[47]

According to Geoffrey, Uther sees a draconic portent in the sky, a dazzling star with a fiery dragon on one of its rays ("globus igneus in similitudinem draconis extensus").[48] Merlin interprets this as signifying that Uther will be king. Uther himself makes two golden dragons, one for his battle standard and one for the cathedral at Winchester. From Uther this dragon is in due course inherited by Arthur.

Unfortunately, the value of these traditions about the old British kings depends entirely upon the reliability of Geoffrey of Monmouth. He claims to have his information from ancient records preserved in a very old British (or possibly Breton) book ("Britannici sermonis librum vetustissimum") which he obtained from Walter the Archdeacon.[49] But even in his own time Geoffrey was regarded as a great liar by other historians, such as William of Newburgh, who says that Geoffrey passed on fables of Arthur as honest history ("fabulas de Arturo . . . honeste historiae nomine palliavit").[50] Gerald of Wales tells of a man troubled by evil spirits, which were banished when the Gospel of St. John was placed upon his chest but returned at once when Geoffrey's *History* was placed there instead.[51] Though a goldmine for popular storytellers, and a force to be reckoned with for centuries, Geoffrey's *History* is notoriously unreliable, and it is especially likely to be fictitious in his account of the glorious reign and fabulous deeds of King Arthur.

Although Geoffrey attributes the dragon device to Arthur, he goes on in the very next passage to describe Arthur's shield as bearing an image of the Virgin Mary ("imago sancte Marie Dei genetricis").[52] In this he agrees with William of Malmesbury (about 1125): "fretus imagine Dominicae matris, quam armis suit insuerat", who follows the much older tradition of Nennius: "Arthur portavit imaginem Sanctae Mariae perpetuae virginis super humeros suos".[53] It may be that Nennius had given Arthur this device in order to ingratiate the wild warrior of British oral tradition with the churchmen for whom he was writing,[54] and it is likely that Nennius or his source had confused Welsh *ysgwydd* ('shoulder') with *ysgwyd* ('shield').[55] But, however it may be with Nennius about 800 A.D., it does appear that Geoffrey of Monmouth in the twelfth century is trying to harmonise an old tradition — that Arthur bore the image of Mary on his arms — with another tradition, that of the old British dragon, which he also wishes to attribute to Arthur.

It has also been suggested that a dragon was associated with the traitor Mordred on account of his name (which resembles *mor-draic*, 'sea-dragon'), while Arthur's own name recalls Welsh *arth,* 'bear', so that Arthur's dream of the killing of a bear by a dragon originally foretold his death at the hands of Mordred. Geoffrey, however, in his treatment of the story, transferred the dragon symbol from the traitor to Arthur.[56] Thus, for Geoffrey and those who read him, the dream became a prophecy of Arthur's coming victory over the Saxons.

For these reasons we may be reasonably sure that the royal Dragon of Arthur, for all its prominence in mediaeval literature, goes back no further than Geoffrey of Monmouth. Nevertheless, Geoffrey's invention was not inappropriate, in view of the importance of the military dragon among the British people and their ancient use of the word 'dragon' to signify a distinguished warrior or war-leader.

As we saw, Geoffrey also attributes to Arthur a father named Uther Pendragon. This, too, has become a firmly established part of the Arthurian tradition. But although, as Rachel Bromwich has shown (pp. 520-521) the name Uthur does occur earlier than Geoffrey, there is absolutely no evidence that Arthur had a father of that name in earlier tradition. Some texts of Nennius interpolate after the name of Arthur the words 'mab uthr', and it may be that Geoffrey, using such a text, understood these words as meaning 'son of Uther'. If so, he was probably mistaken, for *uthr* is an adjective meaning 'dreadful' or 'wonderful' — both attributes appropriate to Arthur — and so the epithet could mean 'dreadful' or 'wonderful youth' or, as Fletcher prefers, 'cruel from his boyhood'.[57] Two thirteenth-century Nennius texts have a gloss which explains the epithet in this way: "(Arthur) mab uter Britannice, filius horribilis Latine".[58] Thus, Arthur's great father, Uther Pendragon, also appears to be a creation of Geoffrey of Monmouth and so to be no older than the twelfth century.

We saw too that Uther's standing epithet 'Pendragon' is understood by mediaeval romance as meaning 'dragon's head' and as referring to Uther's arms: that also goes back to Geoffrey and no further. In fact, *pen dragon* is 'chief warrior' and other men are referred to as *pen draig* or *pen dragon* in early Welsh literature.[59] The form of Uther's epithet may be compared with that of Ysbyddaden, who is called *Pencawr*, 'chief giant', or with the common term *pencerdd*, 'chief poet'. If, as we have seen, Uther was originally not a person but an attribute of Arthur, then his epithet, *pen dragon*, must be applicable to Arthur. And so it is, for Arthur was the chief warrior. It therefore appears that the words of the Nennius manuscripts which read "Arthur mab uthr pen dragon" did not mean 'Arthur, son of Uther Pendragon', but 'Arthur, terrible youth, chief warrior'.

The dragons liberally associated with Arthur thus appear to be fictions deriving from Geoffrey of Monmouth at the beginning of the twelfth century. We can no more draw conclusions from that source than we can from Shakespeare, who has King Lear describe himself as a dragon:

> Peace, Kent,
> Come not between the Dragon and his wrath.

In cases like these, the writer tells us something of the way the ancient kings of Britain were regarded in his time, but he is no witness to that age itself. The only true witnesses we have to the earliest days of Wales are Nennius and the ancient Welsh lays themselves, the *Gododdin* and the authentic verses of Taliesin. Geoffrey tells us only that in his mind, and so probably among some of his contemporaries, the ancient kings of the Britons had been associated with the dragon. The one solid fact that lies behind that association, and explains *why* the Normans thought the Dragon an appropriate emblem for Britain's most famous king, is the demonstrable importance of the dragon in the life and literature of the British people themselves and their habit of using the dragon to signify both the warrior and the nation.

Chapter 3

Norman Conquerors and Welsh Rebels

(i) The Dragon and the Kings of England

The Normans appear not to have used the dragon as a battle emblem at all before Plantagenet times (late in the eleventh century), although their ships still had dragon-ornamented prows, a tradition they derived from their Viking ancestors. Whenever battle dragons are mentioned in Norman literature or shown in Norman art they are emblems of the enemy, like the Saxon dragon on the Bayeux tapestry. The *Chanson de Roland* (about 1080) refers repeatedly to the dragon banner of the Saracen king Marsilies and to the *draconarius* Abismes who bears it. Wild (1962, p.47) quotes the following passages:

> Sun dragon portet à quei sa gent s'alient. (*Ch. de Rol.* 1641)

> Li Amirals mult par est riches hum:
> Devedant sei fait porter sun Dragun
> E l'estandart Tervagan e Mahun
> E une ymagene Apollin le felun. (*Ch.de Rol.* 3265-8; cf. also 2542ff; 3329ff)

> (The Emir is a very powerful man.
> Before him he has borne his dragon
> And the standard of Tervagant and Mahum
> And a statue of Apollyon the wicked.)

This poem was written when the Saracens had seized control of Spain and were threatening France. The poet sees them as heathens, 'paiens' who worship gods and idols; and in the above passage these include Tervagant, Mahomet and Apollyon. Tervagant has not been identified by commentators, who are also undecided as to whether Apollyon means the Greek sun-god Apollo or Apollyon of the New Testament apocalypse (the book of Revelation). Mahomet of course claimed only to be a prophet, but westerners often treated him as a Moslem god. T.A. Jenkins, in his comment on the passage I have quoted, mentions the *Chanson's* reference to the dragon of Baligant, another of the Saracen leaders, and says that it "is no doubt imagined to be like that of Harold on the Bayeux tapestry, a small dragon made of solid wood or metal and fixed at the end of a shaft. It is held by a foot-soldier while the fighting goes on".[1] There is no doubt, then, that, for the Christian author of the *Chanson*, the dragon is an enemy emblem.

In the history of the Norman kings of England there is not one reference to their use of a dragon banner prior to that of Richard I, who displayed it at Messina in 1190 and took it to the Holy Land.[2] After him, his brother John also used the dragon standard.[3] By this time the *History* of Geoffrey of Monmouth had become established and for Norman kings there was a political propaganda advantage to be had by adopting the now well-known insignia of the legitimate ancient kings of Britain.

Thus, some decades after Geoffrey, the dragon was being used by the Plantagenet kings of England, who were struggling to establish and legitimise themselves as heirs to the whole of Arthur's kingdom. The dragon of both Richard and John was an inflatable three-dimensional flying dragon.[4] Henry III, in a mandate of 1244, makes the traditional Red Dragon his own when he directs:

> a dragon to be made in fashion of a standard, of red silk sparkling all over with gold, the tongue of which should be made to resemble burning fire, and appear to be continually moving, and the eyes of saphires or other suitable stones, and to place it in the church of St. Peter, Westminster, against the king's coming.

Under Henry the English bore this Red Dragon against the Welsh in Snowdonia in 1245,[6] when they were suppressing what they regarded as a rebellion (although in fact the English crown had never gained complete control of the area). They bore it again in Henry's campaign against Llywelyn ap Gruffudd in 1257.[7] For Henry the clearest way to symbolise the legitimacy of his own claim to rule the Welsh was to show himself in Wales bearing the Dragon of the kings of Britain.

After the battle of Lewes in 1264, at which Henry III used the dragon standard against Simon de Montfort,[8] we do not hear of its use again by an English king, apart from an isolated report relating to the battle of Crécy in 1346. Here, a flag showing the Red Dragon was displayed together with several others. In all probability it was not in this case the emblem of the English king, but was adopted out of respect for the many Welsh soldiers in the army of Edward of Woodstock, Prince of Wales, who was fighting beside the king.[9]

Thus the Plantagenet kings of England laid claim to the British dragon in order to imply the legitimacy of their own succession to the old British kings who had used that standard before. That very fact shows that by Plantagenet times the national dragon of Britain was well-known as a military and a national symbol. As Schramm shrewdly observes (p.663), the time when we hear of Plantagenet kings using the dragon standard is also the time when that family had a prince called Arthur (the Duke of Brittany, born 1187).

However, since they appear not to have used it after 1264, the English kings evidently lost interest in the dragon banner in the later part of the thirteenth century. It may be that, by this time, the Normans had patently become the aristocracy of England and the conquerors of Wales. It was a time of constant and intense warfare in Wales, and the English kings were by now more concerned with subduing the rebellious Welsh than with presenting themselves as their legitimate rulers.

From the late thirteenth century on, the English conquerors began to express their national sentiment increasingly through a new emblem: the figure of St. George. His association with England appears to derive from the Third Crusade (1189-90), when Richard I placed himself under his protection. The day of St. George (23rd April) was first declared a feast day in England by the synod of Oxford in 1222. The Order of the Garter, which recognises him as its patron saint, was founded in the mid-fourteenth century by Edward III. The English are reported as using the battle-cry 'St. George!' first under Richard, and thereafter at Poitiers (1356), Shrewsbury (1403), Agincourt (1415) and Cravant and Verneuil (1423-24).[10] Henry VII used it at Bosworth Field in 1485. The banner of St. George was used by the English in 1405, 1415 (Agincourt) and 1485 (Bosworth).[11] After the battle of Agincourt the St. George's Day celebrations were prolonged to make a two-day festival, and the King, returning from France, was met on London Bridge with a large figure of the saint, armed and defending the capital.[12]

With the rise of the cult of St. George in England from the late thirteenth century, the Dragon was no longer wanted as an emblem of national unity by the English kings. Furthermore, the saint was above all things a dragon-killer (Figure 12) — a role he had inherited about the eleventh century from the archangel St. Michael;[13] and while the English kings were occupied with endless wars to subjugate the Welsh, the symbolic image of St. George slaying the dragon was for them a most effective symbol of the real conflict between English kings and Welsh rebels.

Use of the Dragon in Wales by Plantagenet kings had failed to persuade the Welsh that the kings of England were their rightful lords; it also failed to prevent them from continuing to use that emblem as their own. Indeed, as the ferocity of their struggle for independence increased, so also did the prominence of the Dragon as the symbol of their independence. As the English increasingly identified themselves with St. George, so the Welsh adhered ever more strongly to the Dragon.

(ii) The Deliverer of the Welsh

Since the beginning of their oppression, the Welsh people had talked of the coming deliverer who would cast off the English yoke. That is evident as early as the tale of the two dragons of Dinas Emrys reported by Nennius, and it accounts for the persistent Welsh belief in the return of Arthur, *rex quondam et rex futurus*. The faith that Arthur had not died, but would come again to restore the glory of his people, was the famous 'hope of the Britons', and it was a serious enough force in history to cause concern to the kings of England. Henry II had what were taken for Arthur's bones exhumed at Glastonbury in 1170, so as to prove that the king of the Britons was truly dead,[14] and King John seems to have arranged the murder, in 1203, of his nephew Prince Arthur of Brittany before he might attempt to acquire the throne of Britain. It is generally agreed that John instigated this misdeed, and that, since his own title to the British throne was uncertain, he feared that Arthur's name alone would bring him support from the Welsh.

The hope of the Britons was not placed in Arthur alone. Other of their ancient heroes, descended, as was supposed, from Brutus, served as well. Geoffrey of Monmouth gave wide currency to the old traditions that Brutus was the grandson of Aeneas of Troy, the hero of Virgil's *Aeneid*; that he came to Britain, founded Troynovant or New Troy (London), and was the progenitor of a long line of British kings, among whom were Lud, Cymbeline, Vortigern, Uther and Arthur. After Geoffrey has had Merlin explain the symbolism of the two fighting dragons we have met in Nennius, Merlin is made to prophesy the future of Britain to the end of the world. He describes events up to the Norman Conquest and the reign of the early Norman kings of England, and says that then Normandy will lose its power: the Britons will defeat Saxons and Normans and again rule the island. To lead them to this victory, the early British heroes Cadwaladr and Cynan will return. Cadwaladr was the king who, according to modern authorities, died of the great pestilence in 664 A.D. Over the centuries, says the historian J.E. Lloyd, he "became a commonplace of the *cywyddau brud*, the darkly phrased poems in which the bards shrouded their incitements to resistance".[15] Griffiths (p.114) thinks that the legend of his return probably took shape soon after his death, and that the Cymry, in the following centuries, quite naturally longed for the return of this last of their great kings, a symbol of their departed glory. As for Cynan, she thinks it impossible to say at what time he became associated with the legend, or even who he was — possibly "some old hero of the north who had lived in the sixth century".[16] At any rate, according to Merlin's prophecy, as given by Geoffrey, "Cadwaladr shall call unto Cynan and shall receive Albany (i.e. Scotland) into his fellowship . . . The island shall be called by the name of Brutus, and the name given by the foreigners shall be done away".[17]

Cynan was associated with Cadwaladr well before the time of Geoffrey, for the return of both leaders is prophesied in the poem 'Armes Prydein' (the 'Prophecy of Britain'), included in the *Book of Taliesin*. This poem "makes use of all the resources of prophetic tradition and brings them to bear on the political situation of about 930", which is therefore its approximate date of composition. It optimistically foretells that Welshmen, leagued with other Celts, will be led to victory over the Saxons by Cynan and Cadwaladr, "the two *meibion darogan* or 'sons of prophecy', who will return from past ages".[18]

There are many such vaticinatory poems which refer to Cadwaladr or to Cynan (or to both) who will return to deliver the Britons,[19] and from the twelfth century onwards the deliverer may be referred to as 'Owain'. This first occurs in a twelfth century prophecy attributed to Merlin, telling of 'Owain', who has been long concealed but will return to conquer all Britain up to London.[20]

The poets and the people constantly looked to their great families, hoping to recognise some present leader who might fit into the role of the promised deliverer. In the twelfth century his naming as 'Owain', rather than Arthur or Cadwaladr, may perhaps have been a compliment to Owain Gwynedd, who earned glory in his wars against Henry II, or it may possibly represent some older tradition, e.g. a reference to Owain ab Urien of the late sixth century. From this time on, poets may bestow the title 'Owain' on some promising contemporary leader, even if his name is not Owain (as with the Robert of Gloucester who was Henry I's illegitimate son, and, later on, Henry Tudor).[21] Association with this Owain of tradition may account for the popularity of that name in the great houses of the time, and it was exploited by such claimants to the deliverer's role as Owain Cyfeiliog of Powys and Owain ap Cadwgan.[22] Griffiths suggests that the fame of Owain Lawgoch (died 1378) enabled 'Owain' to replace Arthur in some traditional legends of the coming deliverer, as when Owain, rather than Arthur, sleeps in a cave with his warriors, awaiting, like the German Barbarossa, the day appointed for his return.[23] Certainly this tradition of an Owain who would come and deliver his people from the English tyranny must have given support to the rebellious efforts of Owain Glyndŵr and Owain Tudor (whose grandson, the victorious Henry Tudor, was known in Wales as 'Owain').[24]

Still more persistent than such personal names as Arthur, Cadwaladr, Cynan or Owain is the term *draig* or *pen draig*, which the prophetic bards so often attach to the coming saviour of the nation, or to the particular rebel of the present time who promises to assume that role. In the earliest of the poems calling him 'Owain', the deliverer (probably Henry I's illegitimate son Robert of Gloucester) is also called 'dreic darogan', 'the foretold Dragon'.[25] The poet Gwalchmai (about 1130-80) refers to his patron, the rebel prince Rhodri ab Owain Gwynedd, as 'pen dreic a phenn dragon', 'chief dragon and chief of dragons'.[26] The promised Owain is often also called 'Lion' or 'Dragon' ('Llew glew Owain', 'Owain ben draic', 'Owain llew rroddiat').[27] The 'dreic owyned', 'Dragon of Gwynedd', referred to in *Anrec Urien*, seems to be Gruffudd ap Llywelyn ap Seisyllt.[28] The Lord Rhys is 'Lion-Dragon' and 'Prince of Dragons'.[29] Hywel ab Owain is 'penn dragon'.[30] In the fifteenth century Sir Rhys ap Thomas is called 'Draig Urien'.[31]

However, while examples of this use of *draig* or *dragon* might easily be multiplied,[32] they do not allow us to assume an exclusive role for the dragon as the emblem of the Welsh nation or its promising leader, for in all this poetry the dragon is but one symbol among others. The long-awaited deliverer may also be called the Lion, the Bull, the Eagle, even the Wolf.[33] The early pseudo-Taliesin poem 'Armes Prydein' calls Cynan and Cadwaladr 'deu arth', 'two bears', and 'bear' is not uncommon in other poems of the kind.[34] We must also remember that the poet, in using the word *draig*, *dragon* may not be thinking of the animal at all. No less an authority than the Wales Herald Extraordinary, Major Francis Jones, has warned us to seek no heraldic significance in these bardic references to 'the Dragon', since that term was commonly no more than a synonym for 'warrior'.[35]

All we may fairly say is that the dragon is among the most prominent of these animal symbols; that it always had been and remained the common term for a great warrior, and that, where it applied to the deliverer of the people, it accorded especially well with the never-forgotten tradition of the Red Dragon of Dinas Emrys as well as with the dragon-banner of

Uther Pendragon, awarded to him and to all the old and true kings of the Britons by Geoffrey of Monmouth. The prophetic poems of the old Welsh bards are admittedly a native tradition and show little sign of direct influence from Geoffrey,[36] but few Welsh patriots after Geoffrey's time could possibly be ignorant of Uther Pendragon, now celebrated even by their enemies and known throughout Europe, while the Red Dragon of the Britons, known already to Nennius, belonged to popular traditions far older than Geoffrey and must have been known to bards and their audiences from native sources. Apart from folk tales, where the story often appears, there was the tale of *Lludd a Llefelys*.

Of all the symbolic beasts found in bardic poetry, the dragon was by now the most clearly and characteristically Welsh. Belonging to no particular region or family, but associated from the most ancient times with the continued struggle for Welsh independence, it was best placed to become the focus of the spirit of patriotic fervour and national rebellion whenever such rebellion might occur.

While the warriors, chiefs and princes of Wales were constantly called 'dragons', we do not have any clear evidence to prove that they ever used a dragon, let alone a red dragon, as a military standard at any time before the fifteenth century. It is perfectly likely that it may have happened, but the literary and historical documents which we have contain no unambiguous reference to the use of a dragon banner by Welsh resistance fighters until 1401 (see below, p.63).

The earliest bardic text which might allow the interpretation that a Welsh leader displayed the dragon as his emblem occurs in the famous elegy on the death of Llywelyn the Last (1282) by Gruffudd ab yr Ynad Coch:

> Pen milwr pen moliant rhag llaw,
> Pen dragon pen draig oedd arnaw;
> Pen Llywelyn deg, dygn o fraw — i'r byd
> Bod pawl haearn trwyddaw.
>
> (Head of a warrior, head of future glory, head dragon with a dragon's head upon him, head of the fair Llywelyn, a grievous fright for the world that it is pierced by an iron pole.)

Llywelyn was of the royal house of Gwynedd, always in the forefront of moves towards independence; chiefs of that house had been 'dragons' since Gildas in the sixth century had called Maelgwn Gwynedd 'insularis draco'. Gruffudd ap Llywelyn ap Seisyllt had been the 'draic owyned' of the *Red Book*; Rhodri ap Owain Gwynedd had been Gwalchmai's 'pen dreic a phenn dragon': Llywelyn the Last's grandfather, Llywelyn Fawr, had been called 'penn dragon' and 'Dragon of Britain' by Prydydd y Moch. Now Gruffudd's tribute to the last ruler of Gwynedd follows the same tradition, calling Llywelyn the 'dragon'. But the vital phrase, "pen draig oedd arnaw", 'he had a dragon's head upon him', need not refer to any symbolic or armorial device. It may simply mean that his head was the head of a warrior. The stanza not inappropriately celebrates Llywelyn's head, for his head had been cut off by order of King Edward I and brought to London, where it was exhibited on a pinnacle of the Tower[37] and crowned with ivy, in mocking allusion to an ancient Welsh prophecy that a Welsh prince would be crowned in London.

Even if we did choose to read that phrase as an allusion to an armorial device, shown perhaps on his shield or helmet, then this *pen draig* must have been the dragon's head which Geoffrey of Monmouth had given to Uther Pendragon and through him to the old kings of Britain. Since the line refers to a dragon's head, not a whole dragon, this could not be the famous Red Dragon which symbolised Welsh independence.

The arms of Llywelyn's father, Gruffudd ap Llywelyn Fawr, were sketched by Matthew Paris (died 1259) and they show, quarterly *or* and *gules* (i.e. gold and red) four lions passant counterchanged.[38] Other arms and seals of that family show the Lions of Gwynedd.[39] Seals of the family show a man in armour on a horse; another seal shows what may be a lion or a boar, but there is no dragon in the arms of Gwynedd. Llywelyn's possible use of the Dragon rests on nothing more than some small ambiguity in the poet's phrase "pen draig oedd arnaw"; there is more reason to suppose that Llywelyn fought under the traditional Lions of Gwynedd, like other leaders of Gwynedd both before and after him, up to Owain Glyndŵr and the Tudors.

Although we cannot show that Llywelyn used the Dragon or was particularly associated with that emblem, it is undoubted that he was an important national leader and we do know that he adopted the title 'Princeps Wallie' in 1258.[40] We also have some reason to suppose that his men wore green and white colours, even though the colours of the princes of Gwynedd were red and gold;[41] for Garmon Jones (p.3) quotes an englyn referring to Llywelyn and his thousand men in green and white:

Mae llu yn Rhosyr, mae llyn — mae eurglych
   Mae f'arglwydd Llywelyn,
  A gwyr tal yn ei ganlyn,
  Mil a myrdd mewn gwyrdd a gwyn.

(There is a host in Rhosfair, there is drinking, there are golden bells. There is my lord Llywelyn and tall warriors follow him; a thousand, a host in green and white.)

These are the colours in which the Black Prince, Edward of Woodstock, was to dress his Welsh contingent at Crécy in 1346: these men were, as D.L. Evans remarked, "the first troops to appear on a continental battlefield in national uniform".[42] Thus, by the middle of the fourteenth century, green and white appear to have been understood as the national colours of Wales; they were to be used later by Henry Tudor as the field for the Red Dragon, and they remain to this day the colours of the national flag, upon which the Red Dragon is set.

With the death of Llywelyn the Last and the execution of his brother David in the following year (1283), the cause of national liberation under leadership of the house of Gwynedd suffered the severest of setbacks. To this weakness of the national cause King Edward I added a further complication when in 1301, at Caernarfon, he declared his own son, Edward, Prince of Wales. This act was received favourably by many of the Welsh, whose interest was not so much in national independence as in having some authoritative prince to appeal to in cases of hardship or injustice.[43] Some 660 of the leading men of the great Welsh families swore homage and fealty to this prince Edward at a number of formal ceremonies in the years 1301-1307.[44] Thus, Welsh loyalties were henceforth divided between those who were true to the new English princes of Wales and those who persevered with the old aspirations of independence.

Those who fought on, or at least continued to hope, still looked for leadership to the house of Gwynedd. The closest legitimate heir to the banner of Llywelyn the Last was the grandson of his youngest brother Rhodri, the famous but elusive Owain Lawgoch.

Owain Lawgoch is believed to be identical with the legendary Yeuain de Galles, who fought against the English king Edward III in his wars in France.[45] The chronicler Froissart tells how Yeuain as a child had been brought to France and educated as a prince by Philip VI, and how Edward III of England had murdered his father and seized his lands.[46] He earned glory by his exploits against the English, particularly at Poitiers (1356) and La Rochelle (1372). He claimed to be by hereditary right the legitimate ruler of all Wales, and his claim appears to have been supported by the King of France.[47]

We know that Owain's threat to Edward III was serious, since a certain Gruffudd Sais suffered the confiscation of his lands in Anglesey on the ground that he was a supporter of "Owain Lawgoch, a traitor and an enemy of the king".[48] In Wales the bards now told of the Deliverer as one who would come from across the sea.[49] There is a poem attributed (wrongly) to Iolo Goch in which the Deliverer appears as a sailor whose two uncles have been killed by the English (as Owain's great-uncles Llywelyn and David had been).[50]

In 1378 Owain was murdered by an Englishman, John Lamb, who was afterwards rewarded by the English authorities.[51] A poem of uncertain authorship tells how the Welsh people had been waiting, armed and ready, for Owain to return and lead the fight.[52] We have already seen how the reputation of Owain Lawgoch was sufficient to enable him to replace even Arthur in the role of the promised Deliverer waiting in his cave for the moment when he should return to lead his people and expel the Saxons. However, while Owain's importance in the aspirations of the Welsh is undoubted, it is not easy to identify the bardic poems which refer to him, since 'Owain' can mean any of a number of promised leaders, and it is not possible to establish any particular connection between Owain and the national Dragon.

With Owain Lawgoch dead, patriots looked again for leadership to the royal house of Gwynedd, and their attention came to focus on another of Llywelyn the Great's descendants, the young Roger Mortimer, Earl of March.

When Roger in 1385 came to be recognised as heir to the English throne, the bard Iolo Goch sang of the joy with which Welshmen looked forward to the crowning of a kinsman of Gwynedd.[53] Plainly recalling the dragons of Dinas Emrys, Iolo declares that it is the blood of the Red Dragon that flows in Roger's veins:[54]

> gwaed y ddraig goch
> yw'r sinobr y sy ynoch.

(The red which is in you is the blood of the Red Dragon)

This is the plainest reference to the traditional Red Dragon of the nation, which the poet now identifies with the nation's leader. In another poem in praise of Roger Mortimer, produced about 1394-98, he refers to Roger as 'dragwn aer' 'the Battle-dragon', 'n draig ni', 'our dragon', and 'draig ynysoedd' 'dragon of the islands', recalling that most ancient epithet of the princes of Gwynedd, 'insularis draco'[55] (cf. above, p.43).

This poet's repeated use of the word 'dragon', together with several references to his kinship with the old princes of Gwynedd and this explicit identification of Roger with the Red Dragon, seems to indicate that Roger's claim to these honours was not so self-evident as Llywelyn's or Owain's had been and therefore needed the art of the poet-propagandist to make it plain. Perhaps it was because he was descended not from the sons of Llywelyn Fawr, but from his daughter Gwladus Ddu, who had married Ralph de Mortimer in 1230. Perhaps, too, Roger had not earned his credentials in the proper way, by spilling volumes of English blood; indeed, far from regarding him as a true rebel, Richard II of England had designated him his successor. But by the time Richard was deposed, Roger had been killed by rebels in Ireland. Roger was a man with a foot in either camp, and to hold the sympathy of the Welsh he needed propaganda, which stressed his descent from the royal house of Gwynedd. A genealogy prepared for that purpose traces the Mortimers through Gwladus Ddu and the house of Gwynedd back to Cadwaladr and Brutus, and it is decorated with a long, two-legged Red Dragon with a blunt tail, plainly intended to symbolise the Welsh descent.[56] If such a man could be accepted as the true heir of Llywelyn and leader of the Welsh, then his eventual succession to the throne of England would resolve the old conflict between the nations and leave both parties satisfied. But it was not to be. Roger Mortimer died in 1398 with Richard II still on the throne of England.

Soon after the death of Roger Mortimer the poets and people of Wales were roused to rebellion again by Owain Glyndŵr, who in 1401-4 succeeded in conquering virtually the whole of Wales.

One of the earliest great successes of his career was his siege of Caernarfon (2nd November, 1401), at which he unfurled his banner, displaying a golden dragon on a white field, as the chronicler Adam of Usk records: "in multitudine glomerosa vexillum suum album cum dracone aureo ibidem displicuit".[57] About the same time he had produced a Great Seal, showing four lions rampant — presumably derived from the old royal arms of Gwynedd from which he claimed descent; we have good reason to believe that his personal shield showed these lions quarterly in red and gold.[58] About 1404 he produced another Great Seal, which he used from that time onward, showing him as an armed mounted warrior on one side and as a sceptred prince on the other: both Owain and his horse are here crested with a wyvern (a heraldic form of a dragon) with raised wings.[59] He also used a dragon, together with a lion, as a supporter on his shield of arms.

Since Owain traced his ancestry to the ancient kings of the Britons (through Cadwaladr to Camber, son of Brutus) and was calling upon the Welsh to rise up against their English oppressors, it is likely that these dragons were intended to recall the dragon of Uther Pendragon. According to Thomas Pennant, writing in the eighteenth century, the golden dragon on a white field which Owain displayed at Caernarfon had been modelled on the 'vexillum aureus draco' of Arthurian tradition:[60]

> Owain to animate his countrymen called up the ancient prophecy which signified the destruction of Henry under the name of the mole, cursed of God's own mouth. Himself he styled the dragon, the name he used in imitation of Uther Pendragon, whose victories over the Saxons were foretold by the appearance of a star with a dragon underneath, which Uther used as his badge and on that account it became a favourite with the Welsh. On Percy he bestowed the title of lion from the crest of the family; on Mortimer the wolf.

The use of a symbolic dragon by and on behalf of Roger Mortimer to advertise his claim to be the legitimate heir of Cadwaladr and leader of the Welsh people had prepared the way for Owain Glyndŵr's choice of the dragon to symbolise the same claim.

From 1404 onward we hear no more of Owain's use of the dragon emblem. It seems that, having become established as Prince of Wales and successor to Llywelyn, he now preferred to display the Lions of Gwynedd.[61] But with his unfurling of the dragon banner at Caernarfon he has given us the first clear example of the use of the Dragon as the emblem of Welsh independence and the spirit of the Welsh nation.

Glyndŵr's military Dragon clearly derives from Geoffrey of Monmouth, who in turn had constructed his story out of earlier British traditions. The continued use of 'dragon' as a term of praise for the warrior chief, and the never-forgotten tale of the red and white dragons of Dinas Emrys, had made it possible for poets, notably among them Iolo Goch, to employ the dragon to express the legitimacy and Welsh patriotism of Roger Mortimer. With the ground thus prepared, Owain Glyndŵr a few years later could display the dragon again to good patriotic effect, choosing in his case not the red dragon of the Welsh people, but the golden dragon of Uther, which suited better his own aspiration to be their prince.

Throughout the Middle Ages the colour of the Dragon fluctuates between gold and red. This, like so much else, is a legacy from Geoffrey of Monmouth, for while the dragon of the Britons seen by Ambrosius is plainly red ('rubeus draco'), the one displayed by Uther Pendragon is gold ('vexillum, aureus draco'). The princes of Gwynedd, whose family colours were red and gold, had no reason to prefer one colour to the other.

One of the earliest references to the coming deliverer, probably from the time of Henry I, describes his banner as red, but does not say whether the emblem is a dragon:[62]

> Lumangoch gwynn vot. leitheu oruot.
> arwyd eudyot. aerwyr eryrot.

Griffiths (p.135) paraphrases this, and the two lines after it, as: 'the eagle-like warriors will have a red banner; there will be ships on the sea; and in the tumult throughout Wales, taxes or high offices will count for naught'. Henry III, usurping the dragon of Britain, had his dragons made in red (cf. above, p.54). Thereafter there is no clear reference to colour for the best part of two centuries, but when Iolo Goch glorifies Roger Mortimer in the 1390's it is the Red Dragon he refers to ("gwaed y ddraig goch/yw'r sinobr y sy ynoch"). Similarly, the dragon depicted in the Mortimer genealogy is mainly red.[63]

Owain Glyndŵr, choosing the dragon of Uther Pendragon rather than that of Ambrosius, displays a golden dragon at Caernarfon, though his family colours were red and gold. Strictly, the golden dragon should symbolise the legitimacy of his descent from Uther and the British kings, while the red dragon represented the independence of the people. Owain, who may have studied law, may have been sensitive to that distinction and may have thought it more important to demonstrate the legitimacy of his own claim rather than his association with the spirit of national independence. At this time the dragons of Ambrosius and of Uther had not yet merged into one. Thus the colour of the 'Welsh' dragon remained as unresolved in the late Middle Ages as it had been in Geoffrey's time.

Chapter 4

The Tudor Dragon and the Modern Symbol of the Welsh Nation

(i) Rebellion: Owain, Edmund, Jasper

With the disappearance of Owain Glyndŵr in the years after 1410 and the reconquest of Wales by the English, who now imposed their rule more thoroughly than before, poets and patriots once again waited hopefully for some new leader to arise, a condition recalled in a verse by Lewis Glyn Cothi:[1]

> Cysgu 'roedd Cymru medd sawl a'i gwyl
> Yn hir heb flaenawr fau ragorawl.
>
> (Wales was sleeping, say those who watch over her,
> Long without a fine leader)

This champion was found in the house of Tudor whose seat was at Penmynydd in Anglesey.

Owain Tudor, like Owain Glyndŵr, claimed descent from the ancient kings of Britain. Whether he also claimed the British dragon, or whether that device was first used by his sons, we do not know; but his sons Edmund and Jasper both used a red blunt-tailed dragon as crest and supporter to the arms granted to them by Henry VI, and Jasper also showed a dragon on his seal.[2] Since the thirty known coats of arms of Owain's ancestors do not anywhere include a dragon or wyvern, we may be sure that the function of this ornament, adopted when the Tudor family had replaced Glyndŵr as leaders of the nation, was to assert the legitimacy of their descent from the old kings of Britain, and perhaps also to show themselves as the representatives of the aspirations of the Welsh people. The poet Dafydd Nanmor certainly has that in mind when, in a poem addressed to the sons of Owain Tudor, he prophesies that the white dragon of the Saxons will soon be overthrown by 'draig velen', the golden dragon of Britain.[3] That hope might seem vain so soon after the suppression of the Glyndŵr rebellion. But for much of the fifteenth century, England itself was torn apart by civil war between the houses of York and Lancaster; and such patriotic bards as Dafydd, though siding generally with the Yorkists, could draw joy and hope from a division of their country's enemy.

When Owain Tudor was executed by Edward IV in 1461, his elder son Edmund having predeceased him in 1456, the hope of the Welsh was quickly transferred to his younger son, Jasper. Already in his elegy on the death of Owain, the poet Robin Ddu o Fôn addresses Jasper and says: "it is time for the Red Dragon to break free":[4]

> Draig wen ddibarch yn gwarchae,
> A draig goch a dyr y cae.
>
> (A white disrespectful dragon laying siege,
> And a red dragon will break the encirclement)

Together with the red dragon of Wales, the red rose of Lancaster is also favoured by Robin Ddu, and he looks forward to seeing 'red roses in high authority' (Rhos cochion mewn rhwysg uchel).[5]

Jasper campaigned long and hard, leading the Welsh Lancastrians against the Yorkist English king. Though repeatedly driven into hiding or exile, he showed great resilience and kept returning to the attack. He earned great praise from the poets, among them Lewis Glyn Cothi, Dafydd Llwyd and Ieuan ap Rhydderch. Deio ap Ieuan Du (c. 1460-80) refers to Jasper's patriotic struggle when he produced the line which was later to become famous as motto of the nation: 'Y draig coch, ddyry cychwyn' (the Red dragon advances).[6] Dafydd Llwyd prophesied that Jasper would give the people a son who will be a dragon of the blood of Brutus.[7] But in the end it was not Jasper, nor his son, but Jasper's nephew Henry Tudor, son of his brother Edmund, who led the rebellion to victory at Bosworth Field in 1485.

Henry Tudor had been born in 1457, after the death of his father. A Tudor chronicler, Ellis Griffith, claimed that the poet Robin Ddu, who had prophesied that Edmund Tudor would one day win back the crown of Britain, was cast into prison when Edmund died sonless, but released when it was learnt that his widow was pregnant. There is, as H.T. Evans noted (pp. 11, 14f), some reason to doubt the reliability of this chronicler, but if his testimony on this matter may be trusted, it illustrates the importance of the bards in maintaining the struggle for independence.[8] Later, during the reign of the Tudors, the Welsh nobles became increasingly Anglicised, so that the bards, dependent as they were on them, dropped their hostility to England. This meant that, during the Civil War, both bards and gentry, and indeed ordinary Welsh people, were alike royalist. But as the bards did not abandon their native tongue, their connection with the (Anglicised) gentry became looser, and their political function — for a time — much reduced.[9]

Not only the Lancastrian Tudors but also the House of York claimed descent from the ancient kings of Britain — through Llywelyn Fawr and his daughter Gwladus Ddu — and they also had support from some of the bards, including Lewis Glyn Cothi and Guto'r Glyn.[10] But the Yorkist King Richard III was highly unpopular: his wars had done great damage, especially in Wales, and his murder of the princes in the Tower — both of them regarded as directly descended from Brutus the Trojan — soon alienated the Welsh Yorkists. Thereafter Henry Tudor became the focus of Welsh patriotic fervour, and he promised to restore to the Welsh people — to quote his own words — "their erst libertyes, deliv'nge them of such miserable servitudes as they had pyteously longe stand in".[11] The bards worked well to unite the people behind their new champion, building up his reputation and feeding expectations of his return from France, where he had lived as an exile after spending his boyhood with his uncle Jasper at Pembroke Castle. Lewis Glyn Cothi became an ardent propagandist in his cause, but in all this poetry, though it is full of animal symbolism, it cannot be said that Henry is particularly associated with the dragon. Indeed, the sign by which he is most often named is 'the Bull'.[12] Sometimes the poets, mindful of his exile abroad, called him 'the Seagull'.[13]

Henry's principal concern when he landed in Wales was of course not to redeem the Welsh from servitude, but to claim what he considered to be rightfully his — again in his own words, "the adeption of the crown unto us of right appertaining".[14] Likewise, not all the Welsh who supported him hoped, with the bards, for supremacy over the English. Some thought that, by placing a Welshman on the throne, they would be more likely to enjoy the privileges of Englishmen.[15]

(ii) Bosworth and After

When Henry Tudor with his allies faced King Richard III at Bosworth, one of his three battle standards showed "a red firye dragó beaten vpó white and grene sarcenet".[16] Upon white and green, the colours of all Wales, he had set the Red Dragon of Welsh popular tradition. After his victory Henry rode with these three standards to St. Paul's cathedral in

London, where they were blessed: they are described thus in the *Chronicle of London*, referring to 27th August, 1485:[17]

> oon was of the Armys of Seynt George, the secund a
> Red ffyry dragon peyntid upon white and Grene Sarcenet,
> and the third was a Baner of Tarteron bett wyth a dun cowe.

Thus, side by side, Henry honoured St. George of England, the Red Dragon of Wales, and the family arms of the Lancastrian house of Beaufort. Another chronicler tells of Henry's standard showing a Red Dragon passant, breathing flames, upon a field divided horizontally green and white, with a background of flames, white and red roses and golden fleurs-de-lis.[18]

The prominence of the Red Dragon as a battle standard at Bosworth and on Henry's entry into London was clearly meant to identify him as the representative of the Welsh people, a true heir of Cadwaladr, Arthur and Brutus, returning to claim his kingdom. Henry had appealed for support to the Welsh, and their support had given him the victory. The dragon, which for so long had been associated with their national leaders, was not his sign, but theirs. Henry himself might have been 'the Bull' or he might have sported the Lions of Gwynedd; but by displaying the Red Dragon and honouring it after the victory, he paid tribute to the Welsh nation that supported him, as Owain Glyndŵr before him had displayed the Dragon, rather than his own Lion, when he rose up as leader of the Welsh people at Caernarfon.

The Red Dragon continued to be prominent in the early part of Henry's reign as Henry VII. In a context where he is stressing its importance for this sovereign, Glanmor Williams observes: "High on that eastern window of King's College Chapel, Cambridge, itself a shrine of the early Tudor myth, the Red Dragon occupies a place of supreme honour over the head of Christ crucified".[19] It figures amongst the decorations for Henry's coronation celebrations, during which he instituted a new pursuivant and named him 'Rougedragon'. His queen, Elizabeth of York, began her coronation festivities with a procession of barges from Greenwich to the Tower of London, one of them displaying "a great red Dragon spowting flamys of fyer into Temmys".[20] At Henry's coronation banquet, the King's Champion rode a horse trapped with "Cadewaladras armes" — though these, as Anglo has noted, will have been "azure, a cross patée fitchée or," and not the red dragon which was confusedly assigned to Cadwaladr long after his time.[21] At Worcester, plans were made to welcome the king with a speech alluding to the prophecy in Geoffrey of

Monmouth's *History* concerning the triumph of Cadwaladr's lineal descendants.[22] Henry himself appears to have taken an interest in promoting his image as the true heir of Cadwaladr and thus of the ancient British kings, since he set up a commission (about 1490) to enquire into the pedigree of his grandfather Owain Tudor. Its members "drew his perfect genelogie from the ancient kings of Brytaine and the Princes of Wales, and so returned their commission."[23] Several other texts from Henry's reign also set forth this descent, and a full account of it, together with the moral that, in Henry, the prophecy to Cadwaladr of the ultimate triumph of Britons over Saxons has been fulfilled, is contained in the *Historia Regis Henrici Septimi* of Bernadus Andreas, whom Anglo describes as "virtually the official historian of the reign" (1961, p.24).

Henry named his first son Arthur and chose Winchester for his birth — a place of importance in Arthurian tradition. Geoffrey of Monmouth had told that Uther Pendragon deposited a golden dragon in this the metropolitan church of his kingdom.[24] Then as now, Winchester could display 'Arthur's Round Table'. It presumably originated as a representation of the wheel of fortune, and, from the material assembled by Anglo (1961, pp. 28f), it seems likely that Winchester had possessed it from the thirteenth century. Although the court poets pointed to Arthurian tradition when they mentioned the naming of the new Crown Prince, it is very striking that not one of them referred to the British descent of the Tudors in this connection.[25] This suggests that concern to claim their descent from the ancient British kings was somewhat half-hearted.

The Prince celebrated his marriage in 1501 with dragon signs,[26] but, after his death the following year, the cult of Arthur naturally fell into disuse, and the red dragon became a rarity — although it was displayed, with other banners, on ceremonial occasions, and appears about 1520 in two illustrated manuscripts on the ancestry of Henry VIII.[27] The quantity of relevant genealogical material even from the reign of Henry VII is not impressive, and this leads Anglo to conclude (1961, p.26) that Henry's own interest in this ancient British ancestry was not great. It is indeed remarkable that a roll pedigree of his son Arthur shows the Prince as true heir to the British kings through his mother, Elizabeth of York, rather than through Henry Tudor. The rolls which Anglo examined show less concern to establish this ancestry for Henry Tudor than for the Yorkist house of Mortimer and for Edward IV (d. 1483) whose ancestors are repeatedly given such compliments as 'heres cadwaladri', 'verus heres

Cadwalladro qui vocatur Rubeus Draco'. A chronicle which describes Edward, with all his ancestors, as 'Rubeus Draco', while the true Saxon line is 'Albus Draco',ends with the claim that the returning 'Rubeus Draco' is Edward IV.[28]

However, the obvious value of the pedigree for any aspirant to the crown made it essential for Mortimer and other Houses to make maximum capital out of their claim, and the documents produced to support them should not obscure for us the importance of the same claims also for Henry VII. It may be that the propaganda effort was greatest where the case was least certain, and it is likely that, once Henry's position was secure and his ancestry acknowledged, he had less cause to press his claim further. This security is surely the reason why his Tudor successors on the throne did not press the matter. Kendrick observes that neither Henry VIII nor Elizabeth I took offence even when the historicity of King Arthur was attacked, and that the former, "whose personal background at the field of the Cloth of Gold was made magnificent with impressive Arthurian figure-paintings", nevertheless "allowed Polydore Vergil, unreproved by royal rebuke, to publish and republish a book in which King Arthur was treated with an unpleasantly critical historical candour" (p.42).

The dragon served as a supporter in the arms of every Tudor sovereign except Mary. She, when bearing her arms conjoined to those of her husband, Philip II of Spain, replaced her dragon with his black eagle. Even for the other Tudors, emblems other than the dragon became more important, and as early as Henry VIII a silver cockerel — *gallus* after *Galles*, Gallia — was used as an emblem for Wales.[29] In Tudor manuscripts, the dragon, alike as badge and supporter, was painted with head, back and wings of red, and the underparts gold.[30] Elizabeth I had the supporting dragon in her arms coloured completely gold.[31] This can be justified from Welsh tradition, where it could occur in yellow, golden or fiery colour. As we saw, Dafydd Nanmor prophesied the victory of the 'yellow' or 'golden' dragon in one of his poems. However, the red colour, evidenced in the earliest traditions, was not entirely supplanted. At Elizabeth's funeral, the standard carried by Lord Bourchier displayed a red dragon passant with raised wings and a barbed tail.[32]

After Elizabeth's death, the dragon was replaced in the royal arms by the Scottish unicorn of the Stuarts. But in many royal seals, the dragon remained in use after Tudor times;[33] and Cromwell brought it back as a supporter in the arms of the commonwealth, probably because he did not want the unicorn there as reminder of the House of Stuart.

Throughout the sixteenth century, the dragon was regarded primarily as the emblem of the Tudor family, and its ancient British aspect was largely forgotten.[34] Wild notes how even old King Arthur became entirely Christianised: in Spenser's *Faerie Queen* (1596) he still wears a helmet adorned with a ferocious dragon, in imitation of Tasso's portrait of the heathen Sultan; but in Drayton's *Polyolbion* (1622), "the sacred virgin's shape he bore for his device", and no dragon is mentioned.[35]

After Bosworth, the Welsh gentry flocked to London for their rewards, and acquired positions at court or in the business world. All this inevitably brought the two countries closer together. In 1504 Henry granted a Charter of Liberties to Gwynedd and "began the work of uniting Wales with England which his son Henry VIII completed with his Act of Union", which brought Welsh MPs to Westminster.[36] On the other hand, Elizabeth's Act ordering the translation of the Scriptures into Welsh did more than any other single factor to preserve the Welsh language and so enable Wales to retain a separate identity.[37] Not that these were her aims. The Act was passed because she and her ministers feared that ignorance of the Scriptures would weaken Welsh resistance to Catholic teaching and so favour the kind of Catholic rising which was long an ever-present danger to the throne. As has been said, apropos of Elizabeth's Act: "The Tudors were practical politicians, not liberal and enlightened statesmen."[38]

(iii) The Red Dragon of Modern Wales

In Wales, where the red dragon has long been keenly felt as a national symbol, it could not become the emblem of any single princely family. There is no dragon in the arms of Welsh nobility of the fourteenth century, and this has not changed subsequently. Sir Anthony Wagner gives coloured illustrations of the arms of thirty-six royal and aristocratic Welsh families, all without a dragon.[39] Owain Glyndŵr used it only temporarily, and even the Tudors used it only as a supporter. The powerful princes who had the dragon as a banner had other personal emblems — the bear, the lion, the Virgin Mary, and others. The arms of Llywelyn, with four lions, became the emblem of the princes of Gwynedd at least as early as the mid-thirteenth century, and was presumably adopted by Owain Glyndŵr for this reason.[40] It became the special emblem of the Princes of Wales and is in use today in the arms of the prince.

Only when an individual represented the aspirations of the whole nation could he be linked in popular tradition with the red dragon; and for this reason both sides in a political conflict might claim the dragon: Plantagenet kings and Welsh rebels, the Tudors and the House of York. Lewis Glyn Cothi praised Gruffudd Ieuan Llwyd (who welcomed Henry when he landed near Milford Haven and accompanied him to Bosworth Field), denoting his valour thus:[41]

> a gwns ynghylch maner goch,
> a ffyrdd uthr ffordd yr aethoch.
>
> (and guns around a red banner
> and terrible pathways the way you went)

In Wales, then, the dragon is not the personal emblem of princes or kings, nor, as in China, a symbol of the monarchy, but a national symbol reserved for representatives of the whole people and for legendary kings who stood for the lost national splendour.

Modern nationalism arose in Wales, as elsewhere, in the nineteenth century,[42] and continues to gain strength in a situation where the Welsh feel their cultural heritage threatened by growing anglicisation. The most recent census showed that Welsh speakers comprise only 20% of the population, as against 26% in 1961. As the cultural community shrinks in size and becomes painfully aware of the threat to its identity, so nationalist feelings become more intense.[43]

The red dragon has once more asserted itself in this period of growing nationalism. In 1807, after the union of the parliaments of Great Britain and Ireland, it was declared that 'a red dragon passant standing on a mound should be the king's badge for Wales'. And about a hundred years later, Edward VII assigned this badge, differenced with a silver label, to the Prince of Wales.[44] However, it was argued that the heir to the Crown ought to bear some symbol of the principality in his arms, and not merely as a badge; and so in 1911 George V ordained that Prince Edward and his successors as Prince of Wales should set in the centre of their princely shield a small shield, with the lions of Gwynedd.[45] Thus the prince of Wales now has the royal arms with the arms of the principality on an inescutcheon. Then, in 1953, Queen Elizabeth II decreed that the royal badge for Wales should be augmented, and to its red dragon there was added the famous motto 'Y ddraig goch ddyry cychwyn' (cf. above. 67).

This augmented badge was placed on a white flag and flown over government buildings on appropriate occasions. But in 1958 the Gorsedd of Bards expressed the wish that the Red Dragon flag be recognised as the national flag of Wales, instead of this augmented badge. Accordingly, in 1959 Her Majesty commanded that in future "only the Red Dragon on a green and white flag should be flown on Government buildings in Wales and in London, where appropriate". The augmented badge was to continue in use for other purposes, i.e. for its display as a badge in accordance with established heraldic procedure.[46]

In the 1890s representations were made to the crown by Welsh societies to the effect that the Royal arms could accommodate the Red Dragon by dropping one of the golden leopards; and in 1910 Welsh local authorities unsuccessfully petitioned George V to introduce the Dragon both into the Royal Standard and into the coinage of the realm.[47] Major Francis Jones, Wales Herald Extraordinary, and himself of course a Welshman, having noted that, at the time of writing (1969), letters still appear in the press complaining that Wales is not represented in the royal arms, commented:

> Neither are the English represented, because the leopards are those of Anjou, the tressured lion belongs to Scotland, the harp to Ireland. However, the excluded Welsh and English may console themselves with the knowledge that the one still possesses the dragon and the other the cross of the saint who slew it (p.178).

The red dragon is certainly the best known symbol in Wales today. When, about twenty years ago, Esso produced the slogan 'there's a tiger in my tank', the filling stations of the firm in Welsh-speaking Wales handed out a sticker: 'Mae gennyf Ddraig yn fy nhanc' ('I've a dragon in the tank'). But in spite of such trivialising of the symbol, the old dragon can still spit fire, and represents militant as well as other elements in the nationalist movement which aims at a considerable degree of political independence from England. The organ of the Welsh Language Society (Cymdeithas yr Iaith Gymraeg) is called 'Tafod y Ddraig', tongue of the dragon. Welsh writers who do not know Welsh point out that the dragon in fact has two tongues.[48] And the dragon remains the symbol of national consciousness for the people that has been driven by the Anglo-Saxons into the Western uplands.

Notes

For full details of references given in abbreviated form, see p.7 above.

Chapter 1: The Dragon in Prehistory and in Ancient History

1. See Carl Sagan, *The Dragons of Eden*, London, 1977, p. 138. David Attenborough tells of catching a Komodo dragon in his *Zoo Quest for a Dragon*, London, 1957, with splendid photographic illustrations. The term 'monitors' originated because the Egyptian representative of this group of lizards is known to the natives by the name of 'ouaran', which appears to be the Arabic word for all lizards. Transliterated as 'waran', this was confused with the German 'warnen', to warn, whence these reptiles were known as 'Warn-Eidechsen' (warning lizards). Thus the name 'monitors', although a misnomer, is 'too well established to be superseded' (R. Lydekker, *The Royal Natural History*, vol. 5 (Reptiles), London and New York, 1896, p.150.) Lydekker wrote before the Komodo representative of the group had been discovered.

2. The universality of dragon lore is well known. See, for example, Allen and Griffiths, Huxley, Ingersoll; also Elliott Smith, especially pp.83ff, 'The Dragon in America and Eastern Asia'; and Janet Hoult, *Dragons, their History and Symbolism*, Glastonbury, 1990.

3. Visser, having said that Chinese ideas on the dragon have remained unchanged from the remotest times (p.38), quotes Wang Fu, who lived in the time of the Han dynasty, as saying: 'If a dragon has no *ch'ih muh*, he cannot ascend to the sky' (p.70). This seems to be a staff which the animal grasps (Cf. Barber and Riches, p.51). Nevertheless, Chinese lore includes winged dragons, the offspring of the bird *yü-kia* ('the winged barbel', Visser, p.72). In any case, says Visser, the dragon in China has unlimited capacity to transform himself (p.126). As for Japan, in the oldest annals dragons are mentioned 'mostly as water gods', often serpent-shaped; but Indian and Chinese ideas on the subject were soon introduced (p.135).

4. Konrad von Mengenberg, *Buch der Natur*, edited by F. Pfeiffer, Stuttgart, 1861, p.269, 11.18ff. Other late mediaeval

75

encyclopaedias of zoology, such as Konrad Gesner's *Historia Animalium* (5 volumes, Tiguri, 1551-1587), also include data about the nature and habits of the dragon, which is described in the same way as other animals. See also Rudolf Wittkower, '⸀Marvels of the East. A Study in the History of Monsters', *Journal of the Warburg and Courtauld Institutes*, 5 (1942), 159-197.

5. On this and many similar reports, see Ralph Whitlock, *Here be Dragons*, London, 1983, pp. 56-59.

6. Hence the 'money spider', an omen of good fortune. Cf. the saying 'If you wish to live and thrive/Let the spider run alive'. For more examples see Edwin and Mona A. Radford, *Encyclopaedia of Superstitions*, London, 1948, under 'spider'; or H. Bächtold-Stäubli, *Handwörterbuch des deutschen Aberglaubens* (10 volumes, Berlin and Leipzig, 1927-1942), under 'Spinne', especially item 6 (j), 'Spinne nicht töten' (vol. 8, col. 276).

7. Allan and Griffiths, pp. 90-91, 126, following Carl Sagan, as cited in note 1 above.

8. Simpson notes (p.15) that those who, in spite of this enormous time gap, cling tenaciously to the equation between dragon and dinosaur are reduced to supposing that some 'racial memory' of the latter has been inherited by man from his remote non-human ancestors, the primitive mammals contemporary with the dinosaurs. But these mammals were no more than 'small squirrel-like insect-eating creatures, very similar to the present-day Asiatic tree-shrew in size, habits and brain capacity . . . To think that we can 'remember' their experiences of 60 million years ago is wilder than the wildest myth'.

9. The rhinoceros skull is that of *Coelodonta antiquitatis* (Blumenbach): see Otto Schindewolf, *Grundfragen der Paläontologie*, Stuttgart, 1950, text to Tafel I.

10. Ingersoll, pp. 28ff, who refers here to the views of Elliott Smith.

11. Information about beasts from Iranian and Indian mythology was copied from the Royal Archives of Persia by the Greek scholar Ctesias in the fifth century B.C. and similar data were

collected in the time of Alexander the Great by the Greek Megasthenes. (See Wittkower, as cited in note 4 above, pp. 161f). Their reports became part of the lore of Greece. On the transmission of these traditions to mediaeval Europe, and on mediaeval faith in them, see my article 'On Mediaeval Credulity', in *'Erfahrung und Überlieferung'. Festschrift for C.P. Magill*, edited by H. Siefken and A. Robinson, Cardiff, 1974, pp. 5-21.

12.   Sälzle, p. 280.

13.   Ingersoll, p.14: 'It is plain that, in common with the more intelligent animals, man's predominant sensation was fear — fear of his brutish fellows, dread of the jungle and its beasts and ogres, of the desert and its burning drouth, of the wind and the thunderous lightning; most of all terror of the dark, peopled with spirits good and bad. Against the unknown and therefore frightful shapes and noises of the night, the shrieks of the gale, awe of the ocean, the flickering lights and sickening miasma of the bog — all to his half-awakened mind evidence of animate beings above his reach or understanding — man knew of but one defense, which was humble propitiation and never-ceasing payment of ransom. Ghosts blackmailed him throughout his terror-stricken life.'

14.   'There be some Dragons which have wings and no feet, some again have both feet and wings, and some neither feet nor wings, but are only distinguished from the common sort of Serpents by the combe growing upon their heads and the beard under their cheeks.' (Topsell, p.705).

15.   Quoted by J. Franklyn, *Shield and Crest*, third edition, London, 1967, p. 153. An equally detailed and in some respects similar description of the Chinese dragon is quoted by Allen and Griffiths, p. 34.

16.   'There are often heavy rains; and those who speak about these rains say: "Fine moistening rain is heavenly rain, violent rain is dragon rain," ' (Wang Fu, quoted by Huxley, p. 59).

17.   *GPC* under 'Draig (d)'.

18.   Quoted by Visser, p.65: Cf. Elliott Smith, pp. 95-96.

19.   Gregory of Tours, *Hist. Franc.* X, 1, tells of 'magno dracone in modo trabis validae' ('like a thick beam'), seen, accompanied by numerous serpents, in the Tiber during the floods at Rome in 589. Wild (1962, p.10) says that Paulus Diaconus repeats this, in part verbatim, in his *History of the Langobards.*

20.   Topsell, p. 701: 'Among all the kindes of Serpents, there is none comparable to the Dragon, or that affordeth and yeeldeth so much plentiful matter in History for the ample discovery of the nature thereof.'

21.   Ingersoll, p.64. The old Chinese text, a kind of encyclopaedia, may also be spelt 'Shanhaijing'.

22.   Macrobius, *Saturnalia*, 1, 20, 3 (p.112 of J. Willis' edition, Lipsiae, 1963).

23.   Migne, *Patrologia Latina*, vol. 51, columns 835-836.

24.   Martial xii, 53, 3: 'Incubasque gazae ut magnus draco, quem canunt poetae custodem Scythici fuisse luci'; quoted, together with Macrobius and Prosper Aquitanus (cf. notes 22 and 23 above), by Martin P. Nilsson, 'The Dragon on the Treasure', in *Opuscula Selecta*, volume 3, Lund, 1960, pp.117-118 and notes.

25.   In this capacity the dragon ('lung') is called 'fu-ts' ang lung' (i.e. dragon of hidden treasures, watching over the wealth concealed from mortals: Ingersoll, p.46); cf. Barber and Riches, p.52.

26.   Hesiod, *Theogony*, 11. 820-868.

27.   See Fontenrose, especially pp. 13-22 and p.59. On the combat of Zeus and Typhon see pp. 70-76. Typhon is described by Hesiod (or by an early interpolator into his text) as a grotesque reptilian monster, but referred to as δράκων.

28.   Fontenrose, pp. 121-129.

29.   Fontenrose, pp. 148-151.

30.   See Allen and Griffiths, pp. 57-60.

31.   See Allen and Griffiths, p.46, who quote P.B. Lum, *Fabulous Beasts*, London, 1952.

32.   Allen and Griffiths, pp. 15-16. Old Testament passages which actually mention dragons are listed and discussed by Theodor H. Gaster, *Thespis. Ritual Myth and Drama in the Ancient Near East*, New York, 1950, pp. 145-150.

33. See Gertrud Schiller, *Iconography of Christian Art*, London, 1972, vol. 2; text p. 62, and Fig. 213.

34. Peter Paulsen, *Drachenkämpfer, Löwenritter und die Heinrichsage*, Köln, 1966, pp. 52ff.

35. 'Of all the birds the Eagle alone has seemed to wise men the type of royalty, a bird neither beautiful nor musical nor good for food, but murderous, greedy, hateful to all, the curse of all, and with its great powers of doing harm only surpassed by its desire to do it.' (quoted by C.W. Scott-Giles, The *Romance of Heraldry*, London, 1965, p.77).

36. Sälzle (pp. 452-453) says that the divine couple Shiva-Pashuputi were depicted with all the attributes of the jungle — tigers, elephants, serpents — but these were divested of all that was terrifying about them.

37. Isidore, *Etymologiae*, xii, 4, 4 and 6 ('De Serpentibus', ad. init.): 'Draco maior cunctorum serpentium, sive omnium animantium super terram'; and the basilisk is 'rex serpentium'.

38. *Oneirokritika, ii*, 13.

39. Cf. Sälzle, pp. 260-261. The strong association of the dragon with the Emperor is firmly established in the *I Ching* of the twelfth century B.C.

40. The Chinese dragon, says Visser (p.38) has always been a water animal, akin to the snake, which sleeps in pools during winter (the dry season in China) and arises in spring. 'It is the god of thunder, who brings good crops when he appears in the rice fields (as rain) or in the sky (as dark and yellow clouds).'

41. Nennius' association with the *Historia Brittonum* is well attested, though in truth he cannot now be regarded as the work's original compiler: David N. Dumville has given evidence that the ascription to Nennius 'is no older than a Welsh recension of the text in the mid-eleventh century', and that the real author remains unknown, the only indication of authorship being in a prologue of 'Nennius' absent from the best MSS. ('"Nennius' and the *Historia Brittonum*", *Studia Celtica*, x/xi (1975/76), 78-95).

42.   The *Mabinogion* is a modern title for eleven stories preserved in
        two Welsh MS. collections: *The White Book of Rhydderch* (Llyfr
        Gwyn Rhydderch), written c. 1350 A.D., and the *Red Book of
        Hergest* (Llyfr Coch Hergest), c. 1382-1410 A.D. These eleven
        stories probably existed in their present written form by 1250
        A.D. (Griffiths, p. 26). All eleven are rendered in the English
        translation *The Mabinogion* by Gwyn Jones and Thomas Jones,
        London, 1949, (Everyman's Library edition).

Chapter 2: The Dragon of Britain

1.   J. Hastings, *Encyclopaedia of Religion and Ethics*, vol. 3,
        Edinburgh, 1910, col. 297a (art. 'Celts') and 413b (art. 'Charms,
        Amulets, Celtic'); vol. 11, Edinburgh, 1920, col. 404b (art.
        'Serpent-Worship'); J.A. Macculloch, *The Religion of the
        Ancient Celts*, Edinburgh, 1911, pp. 211-212; also Trevelyan,
        pp. 165ff, and Gwyn Jones, pp. 83ff.

2.   Jan de Vries, *Keltische Religion*, Stuttgart, 1961, pp. 167-170
        ('Der Gott mit der Schlange'), discusses fifteen such
        representations from Gaul alone. Cf. also Anne Ross, *Pagan
        Celtic Britain. Studies in Iconography and Tradition*,
        London/New York, 1967, pp. 153-154 and 344-345.

3.   Haverfield and Macdonald, pp. 239-241. The La Tène culture
        (named from archaeological discoveries at this Swiss locality
        beside Lake Neuchâtel) is of Early Iron Age (after that of
        Hallstatt), representing the period of the greatest flourishing of
        the Celts in Europe, before they were constrained by the
        advance of the Romans from the south and Germanic tribes
        from the north. Details in Jan Filip, *Celtic Civilization and Its
        Heritage*, second, revised edition, Wellingborough and Prague,
        1977.

4.   Haverfield and Macdonald, *loc.cit.* Cf. R.W. de F. Feachem,
        'Draconesque Fibulae', *Antiquaries Journal*, 31 (1951), 32-44.
        Most of these brooches belong to the first and second centuries
        A.D.

5.   See I.M. Stead, 'Celtic Dragons from the River Thames',
        Antiquaries Journal, 64 (1984), 269-279, with a full bibliography
        of the subject.

6.   'The serpent or snake was regarded by the Druids as a symbol of the renovation of mankind'; for ' the snake casts its skin annually and returns to a second kind of youth. Fine specimens of this reptile were kept by the Druids close under the altar of Augury, and from their motions important divinations and legal decisions were made' (Trevelyan, p. 170).

7.   D.J. Davies, 'Baner y Ddraig Goch', *Y Fflam* 6, Medi (i.e. September), 1948, p.4

8.   Trevelyan, pp. 170-171. Also *GPC*, under 'glain' and 'maen'.

9.   Ross, as cited in note 2 above, pp. 154, 346.

10.   Geoffrey of Monmouth, *Historia Regum Britanniae*, vii, 4; Griffiths, p.60.

11.   Gwynn Jones, p.83; also Elissa R. Henken, *Traditions of the Welsh Saints*, Bury St. Edmunds, 1987, p.118.

12.   Gwynn Jones, p.84; Henken, as cited in the previous note, pp. 190-191.

13.   *GPC* under 'Draig (d)', 'sheet-lightning', 'lightning unaccompanied by thunder', 'meteorite'. Lights in the sky, such as the aurora borealis, were seen as fiery dragons throughout Britain (cf. Simpson, p.114).

14.   Trevelyan, pp. 165ff.

15.   Gwynn Jones, pp. 83-86.

16.   Pauly-Wissowa, under 'Draco (2)'.

17.   Illustrations of these parts of Trajan's Column may be seen in the two volumes of Plates published simultaneously with Conrad Cichorius' two volumes entitled *Die Reliefs der Traianssäule*, Berlin, 1896 and 1900: Plate xxiii (picture xxxi, section 75); Plate xli (picture lix, section 144); Plate lvii (picture lxxviii, section 204). Descriptions of these are given in the second of the two text volumes, pp. 146, 270, 369ff.

18.   Pauly-Wissowa, *loc.cit.*; also Wild (1962), p.8.

19.   Vegetius, *Epitoma Rei Militaris*, ii. 13; cf. also i, 20-22; ii, 7; iii,5.

20.   Amm. Marcellinus, *Rerum Gestorum Libri*, xvi, 10, 7 and xvi, 12, 39 (Text and translation in the Loeb Classical Library,

edition in 3 volumes, London and Cambridge (Mass.), 1935, vol. 1, pp. 244-245, 284-286).

21.   Gesner, as cited above in note 4 to Chapter 1, vol. 5 (1587), facing p.50 in section H of *De Dracone;* Topsell, p. 702.

22.   Sidonius, Loeb Classical Library edition (cf. note 20 above); text and translation in the first volume (1963): *Poems, Letters, Books i-ii,* poem 5 ('Panegyric on Maiorianus'), 11. 402-407 (p.96).

23.   Tatlock, p.227. Schramm, p.660, noting in this context that such military banners were generally meant to inspire fear, quotes the Norse kenning *lëodbröga,* 'people-frightener', and the term *signa horribilia* used in the Annals of Fulda to signify Norman flags.

24.   Tatlock, *loc.cit.* The passage from *Athis et Prophilias* is also quoted by Du Cange (i.e. Charles Du Fresne, Seigneur Du Cange) in the valuable compilation he gives under 'Draco' in his *Glossarium mediae et infimae latinitatis,* new edition in 10 volumes, edited by L. Favre, Niort, 1883-1887.

25.   J.J. Parry, 'The Historical Arthur', in *Journal of English and Germanic Philology,* 58 (1959), p. 372. Haverfield and Macdonald give details about the Roman army in Britain (pp. 125ff) and about resistance to Saxon invaders (pp. 272ff).

26.   No less an authority than Sir Ifor Williams argued that this sense of the word *draig* derived from the Roman military emblem, by extension from the meaning 'dragon-standard' to signify the man before whom that standard was borne. But there is no pressing evidence for that conclusion. Bromwich (pp. 93-94) prefers to believe that the fighter was called a dragon because his military qualities recalled that beast. In the old literature it is a compliment for a hero to be called a bull, a wolf or a dragon, and the latter became the favourite term for an army leader.

27.   Gildas, *De Excidio Britanniae,* cap. 33-36. In the edition and translation by M. Winterbottom, entitled *The Ruin of Britain* (London, 1978), the Latin is on pp. 102-105, and the English on pp. 32-36.

28.   The decisive publication was Sir Ifor Williams' *Canu Aneirin*, Cardiff 1938. Cf. also Nora Chadwick, *The Celts*, London, 1971, p.285.

29.   *Gododdin*, ed. I. Williams, in *Canu Aneirin*, ll. 243f (p.10): 'Uyg car yng wirwar nyn gogyffrawt/o neb ony bei o gwyn dragon ducawt.' See Kenneth Jackson's comment in his translation, *The Gododdin*, Edinburgh 1969, p. 125.

30.   *Gododdin*, ed. I. Williams in *Canu Aneirin*, 1.298 (p.12): 'dragon yg gwyar gwedy gwinvaeth/gwenabwy vab gwenn; gynhen gatraeth.' Jackson translates: 'the dragon in bloodshed after the wine-feast — Gwernabwy son of Gwën - in the conflict at Catraeth' (p.127).

31.   *Canu Taliesin*, ed. I. Williams, Cardiff, 1960, xii, 1-2. The Welsh text, as edited and annotated in Welsh by Sir Ifor, is given with the introduction and notes in English by J.E. Caerwyn Williams, with the title *The Poems of Taliesin*, published by the Dublin Institute for Advanced Studies, 1968.

32.   John E. Lloyd, *History of Wales from the Earliest Times to the Edwardian Conquest*, third edition, London, 1939, vol. 1, p.230, suggests 664 A.D. as the date of Cadwaladr's death. Griffiths (pp. 112-114) says that Geoffrey of Monmouth dated it at 688 because he confused Cadwaladr with Ceadwalla, King of Wessex.

33.   Griffiths, pp. 107ff, especially pp. 111, 114, 121, 123, 129.

34.   Bromwich, p. 24.

35.   The tale is repeated in Geoffrey of Monmouth's *Historia Regum Britanniae* of about 1136 (certainly before 1139) and in the 'cyfranc' of *Lludd a Llefelys*, where it is fused with another story of the earlier burial of the dragons of Britain on the orders of Llefelys.

36.   Henry of Huntingdon, writing in the twelfth century, reports that Cuthred was preceded into battle by the ealdorman Edelhun, 'regis insigne draconem scilicet aureum gerens.' Henry also says that, in 1016, Edmund Ironside rushed into the fight 'quitting his royal station, which, as was his wont, he had taken between the dragon and the ensign called the Standard': 'loco regio relicto, quod erat ex more inter draconem

et insigne quod vocatur *Standard*' (*Historia Anglorum*, edited by Thomas Arnold, London, 1879, pp. 121, 184). Tatlock (p.225) quotes both passages.

37. Widukind, *Res Gestae Saxonica*, i, 11, says the Saxons had a 'signum . . . sacrum leonis atque draconis et desuper aquilae volantis insignitum effigie' (in *Monumenta Germaniae Historica*, Division 'Scriptores', iii, 422; quoted by Tatlock, p. 224).

38. Williams, *Canu Taliesin*, as cited in note 31 above. The archaic poems are mainly elegies, resembling the *gorchanau* of the *Gododdin*, and most of them are addressed to Urien Rheged.

39. Jackson, as cited in note 29 above.

40. See Schramm, pp. 652-653, who quotes evidence from Carl Erdmann and others.

41. Geoffrey's *Hist. Reg. Brit.*, edited from the Bern ms. by Neil Wright, Cambridge 1984: §168 (p.123), §147 (p.103), §164 (pp. 116-117).

42. Wace, *Roman de Brut*, ed. Le Roux de Lincy, Rouen, 1838, 1.9521. The word 'Brut' meant originally a chronicle or history of the descendants of Brutus, the mythical grandson of the Trojan hero Aeneas, who, according to Geoffrey of Monmouth, conquered giants in Britain and took possession of the land. Arthur was supposedly descended from him.

43. Quoted by F. Jones, p. 169, who also quotes here the passage from Robert Wace.

44. *Ystorya Brenhined y Brytanyeit*, in *Llyfr Coch Hergest*, i.e. *The Red Book of Hergest*, vol. ii, edited by John Rhys and John Gwenogvryn Evans, Oxford, 1890, p. 220 (The volume is entitled *The Texts of the Bruts from the Red Book of Hergest*).

45. Geoffrey, *Hist. Reg. Brit.*, ed. Wright, as cited in note 41 above, §135 (p.95).

46. Layamon of Worstershire's *Brut* or Chronicle of Britain (a poetical semi-Saxon paraphrase of the *Brut* of Wace), 1. 18230 (in vol. ii, pp. 340-341 of Frederic Madden's edition, London 1847).

47. *Le Haut Livre du Graal Perlesvaus*, edited by W.A. Nitze et al, Chicago, 1932, 1. 6590.

48. Geoffrey, *Hist. Reg. Brit.*, as cited in note 41 above, §133 (p.93).

49. *Ibid.*, §2 (p.1). Apropos of the controversy concerning this 'vetustissimus liber' which Geoffrey claimed was his source, Kendrick has observed that 'even today it is not finally decided whether Geoffrey was an outright liar or was telling what might be generously described as a quarter-truth. There was no traditional knowledge that such a long and detailed chronicle about the British kings had been written before Geoffrey's time — the surprise of his contemporaries is proof of this — and there is no allusion to such a work in any surviving historical manuscript known then or thereafter; and, of course, the *vetustissimus liber* itself has disappeared' (p.5).

50. William of Newburgh, in the *proemium* of his *Historia Rerum Anglicarum*, i, 1ff. Kendrick (pp. 11-13) summarises the early criticisms of Geoffrey's book.

51. Gerald of Wales, *Itinarium Kambriae*, bk. 1, ch. 5 (p.58 of the edition by James F. Dimock, London 1868, which forms vol. 6 of *Giraldi Cambrensis Opera* in 8 vols., London, 1861-1891, edited by J.S. Brewer and J.F. Dimock). Cf. also Gerald's *Descriptio Kambriae*, bk. 1, ch. 7 (*vol.cit.*, p. 179), 'sicut fabulosa Galfridi Arthuri mentitur historia' ('as the fabulous history of Goffrey Arthurius falsely maintains').

52. *Hist. Reg. Brit.*, ed. Wright, as cited in note 41 above, §147 (pp. 103-104).

53. William of Malmesbury, *De Gestibus Regum Anglorum*, ed. W. Stubbs, London, 1887, i, 12; Nennius, *British History*, edited and translated by John Morris, London and Totowa (New Jersey), 1980, p.76, sec. 56.

54. Cf. Arthur C.L. Brown, *The Origin of the Grail Legend*, New York, 1943, p. 310.

55. Gerald J. Brault, *Early Blazon. Heraldic Terminology in the Twelfth and Thirteenth Centuries*, Oxford, 1972, pp 24-25.

56. Elaine C. Southward, 'Arthur's Dream', *Speculum* 18 (1943), 249-251.

57. R.H. Fletcher, *The Arthurian Material in the Chronicles*, second edition, New York, 1966, pp. 88-89.

58. Brown, as cited in note 54 above, p. 308.

59.   *The White Book of Rhydderch* (about 1350: cf. note 42 to Chapter 1 above) names a certain 'Wen Bendragon' (Bromwich, *Trioedd* no. 52); the poet Gwalchmai (about 1150) addressed his lord Rhodri ab Owain as 'penn dreic a phenn dragon' (*Red Book of Hergest*, 32, 4). See Bromwich, *loc.cit.*

Chapter 3: Norman Conquerors and Welsh Rebels

1.   T.A. Jenkins, Heath edition of *Chanson de Roland* (revised 1924); comment on 11.3265-8. I owe this information to Prof. Emeritus F. George of the University of Wales.

2.   Richard of Devizes, reporting on King Richard's preparations for the storming of Messina, says: 'The King of England went forth armed; the terrible dragon standard was carried before him unfurled' (Rex angliae, procedit armatus, vexillum terribile draconis praefertur expansum): *De Rebus Gestis Ricardi Primi*, edited by R. Howlett, London 1886, p. 400. (This forms vol. 3 of Howlett's edition of *Chronicles of the Reigns of Stephen, Henry II and Richard I*). Tatlock notes (p.226) that, according to Roger of Hoveden, the next year, on the march in Palestine, there was uncertainty as to who ought to carry the king's ensign, 'draconem suum': see W. Stubbs' edition of Roger's *Chronica* in 4 volumes (London 1868-1871), vol. 3, p. 129.

3.   Tatlock. p. 226, quotes Ralph of Coggeshall (*Chronicon Anglicanum*, Rolls Series, edited by J. Stevenson, London, 1875, p.182) on the use of dragon standards in 1216 by both Louis VIII of France and John of England.

4.   Schramm pp. 662-663, quoting Tatlock's sources, shows that Richard I had an inflatable dragon 'cum capito (sic!) aureo'; and John's was similarly fashioned. The Holy Roman Emperor Otto IV used a three-dimensional dragon at Bouvines (1214), probably to honour his Plantagenet ally. At Crécy, however, an English flag merely bore an image of the dragon, as did the flag of Henry Tudor at Bosworth in 1485.

5.   Tatlock, p. 226, quotes the following instruction given by Henry III to his craftsman Edward, son of Odo: 'Fieri eciam faciat unum draconem in modo unius vexilli de quodam rubeo samitto, qui ubique sit auro extencellatus, cujus lingua sit facta

tanquam ignis comburens et continue apparenter moveatur, et ejus oculi fiant de saphiris vel de aliis lapidibus eidem convenientibus, et illum ponat in ecclesia Beati Petri Westmonasteriensi contra adventum regis ibidem.'

6.   H. Knighton, *Chronicon*, edited by J.R. Lumby, vol. 1 (London, 1889), p. 234: 'signo draconis elevato suos procedere jussit in mortem eorum.'

7.   Tatlock, *loc.cit.*, quotes Matthew Paris, *Chronica Majora* (Rolls Series), edited by H.R. Luard, London, 1880, vol. 5, p. 648: 'vexillum suum regale explicans, quasi draconem, qui nemini novit parcere, exterminium generale Walliae minabatur.' Matthew Paris says that 'to our day' — he died in 1259 — 'the dragon is carried as a *vexillum* before the king in battle' (vol. 1, London 1872, p. 228).

8.   'Acies tamen regalis, quae signo regio, quod draconem vocant, digladiale mortis judicium praetendente, extitit insignita, progreditur' (*Flores Historiarum*, Rolls Series, edited by H.R. Luard, London, 1890, vol. 2. 495. This work is an edition and continuation of Matthew Paris' *Chronica Majora* by various hands).

9.   Tatlock, p. 226, disputes this, saying that the dragon was here the standard of the English king. The source is Geoffrey le Baker's *Chronicon*, edited by Edward M. Thompson, Oxford, 1889, p. 83: 'E contra rex Anglie iussit explicari suum vexillum, in quo draco armis suis togatus depingebatur et abinde fuit nuncupatum *Drago*.'

10.   Tatlock, p. 227: cf. Geoffrey le Baker, *Chron.* as cited in note 9 above, p. 149. Froissart, *Chroniques* (ed. G.T. Diller, Paris, 1972), v, 98-99 (p.61); clii, 108 (p.541); clxxii, 14-30, (pp.595-596); ccxx, 22 (p.714); ccxxvii, 64-65 (p.736).

11.   Tatlock, p. 227, who cites Thomas of Elmham, Thomas Walsingham, Robert Fabyan, J.H. Ramsay and J.H. Wylie.

12.   *Chronicon Adae de Usk*, edited with a translation and notes by Edward M. Thompson, second edition, London 1904, pp. 127-128 (pp. 310-311 for the translation).

13.   The archangel Michael does battle with the Dragon in the New Testament apocalypse, Rev. 12:7ff; cf. also Psalm 91:13, A.V.

(Vulgate 90:13). It has been shown that St. George is represented in the role of the archangel in English art from the late eleventh century (see Wild (1962) p. 50).

14. On Henry's exhumation of the bones of Arthur and Guinevere, see Higden's *Polychronicon*, edited by J.R. Lumby, vol. 5 (London, 1874), p. 333; also Fabyan's *Chronicles*, edited by Henry Ellis, London, 1811, p. 278. Henry also walked over the stone Llech Lavar at St. David's, on which, according to a prophecy attributed to Merlin, an English king would die after conquering Ireland. Gerald of Wales reports that Henry commented: 'Who now will have any faith in that liar Merlin?' ('Merlino mendaci quis de cetero fidem habeat?' *Expugnatio Hibernica*, bk. 1, ch.38; p. 288 in volume 5 of James F. Dimock's edition of Gerald's works, as cited above in note 51 to Chapter 2). Merlin's prophecies, as given in the seventh book of Geoffrey of Monmouth's *Historia Regum*, had told of the ultimate triumph of the British red dragon over the Saxon white one (cf. above, p. 83 n.35), and it was to these prophecies that English chroniclers, such as Higden in the fourteenth century, attributed the restlessness and frequent insurrections of the Welsh. In this connection, Garmon Jones (p. 11) quotes from Higden's *Polychronicon*: 'the prophecy of Merlin and often his witchcraft was wont to beguile them and to move them into battle' ('Hoc consuevit fallere/Et ad bella impingere/Merlini vaticinium/Et frequens sortilegium').

15. J.E. Lloyd, art, 'Cadwaladr' in *Dictionary of Welsh Biography Down to 1940*, edited by himself and others, London, 1959; cf. also Lloyd's *History of Wales, loc.cit.* in note 32 to Chapter 2 above.

16. Griffiths, p. 114. Thomas Parry concurs with her scepticism about Cynan (*History of Welsh Literature*, English translation by H.I. Bell, Oxford, 1955, p. 28). There is a legend about a Cynan known as Cynan (or Conan) Meriadoc, who, late in the fourth century, led an army of Britons to Gaul, where they supported Maximus (Maxen Wledig), defeated the Roman Emperor Gratian and then settled permanently in Armorica.

17. 'Cadualadrus vocabit conanum et albaniam in societatem accipiet . . . Nomine bruti vocabitur insula et nuncupatio

88

extraneorum perebit' (Geoffrey of Monmouth, *Hist. Reg. Brit.*, vii, 3).

18.   A.O.H. Jarman, 'The Later Cynfeirdd', in *A Guide to Welsh Literature*, edited by Jarman and Gwilym Rees Hughes, vol. 1, Swansea, 1976, p. 115.

19.   Griffiths, pp. 86ff; 109ff *et passim*.

20.   *Cyfoesi Myrddin a Gwenddydd*, recorded in the *Red Book of Hergest* (col. 581, 1ff: Ef a gyfyt un orchwech) and in the ms. Peniarth 3 (about 1300); see Griffiths, pp. 99ff.

21.   The 'mab henri' who is identified with 'Owain' in the twelfth century poem beginning 'Llynghes von dirion direidi' (*Red Book of Hergest* col. 1051) is presumably Robert of Gloucester, the illegitimate son of Henry I; see Griffiths, pp. 133-134.

22.   Griffiths, p. 155.

23.   Griffiths, p. 37, quoting John Rhys, 'Welsh Cave Legends and the Story of Owen Lawgoch', *TSC*, 1899-1900, p.1.

24.   See Garmon Jones, p. 37; Griffiths, p. 155.

25.   See the references in note 21 above.

26.   Text in *Llawysgrif Hendregadredd*, edited by John Morris-Jones and T.H. Parry-Williams, Cardiff, 1933, 32, 1.4.

27.   Griffiths, p. 168.

28.   Griffiths, pp. 129-130 (*Red Book of Hergest*, col. 1049).

29.   Thus the poet Cynddelw Brydydd Mawr (about 1155-1200); see also F. Jones, p. 169.

30.   *Ibid.*

31.   *Gwaith Tudur Aled*, edited by T. Gwynn Jones, Cardiff, 1926, vol. 1, p. 78.

32.   Further examples in F. Jones, pp. 169-171, and in the dictionaries under 'draig', 'dragon'.

33.   See Griffiths, pp. 167-170.

34.   Griffiths, pp. 136f.

35.   F. Jones, pp. 171-172.

36.   Cf. Griffiths, pp. 136f.

37.   F. Jones, p. 32.

38.   Matthew Paris, in *Walpole Society Publications*, 14 (1925-26), plate 17 (described on p. 16). See F. Jones, p. 160; also Anthony R. Wagner, *Historic Heraldry*, London, 1939, p. 42.

39.   F. Jones, pp. 158-164.

40.   D. Stephenson, 'Llywelyn ap Gruffydd and the Struggle for the Principality of Wales, 1258-1282', *TSC*, 1983, p. 37.

41.   F. Jones, pp. 158-160.

42.   D.L. Evans, 'Some Notes on the Principality of Wales in the Time of the Black Prince (1343-1376)', *TSC*, 1925-1926, p. 57; cf. A.D. Carr, 'Welshmen and the Hundred Years' War', *The Welsh Historical Review*, 4 (1968), p. 27.

43.   F. Jones, p. 42.

44.   F. Jones, pp. 63-69.

45.   On this see the papers in *TSC*, 1899-1900, by John Rhys, as cited in note 23 above, pp. 1-5, and by E. Owen, 'Owain Lawgoch — Yeuain de Galles: Some Facts and Suggestions', pp. 6-105, together with the correspondence in the volume for 1900-1901 (pp. 87-113).

46.   Froissart, *Chroniques*, edited by J.A.C. Buchan, Paris, 1835, i, 640 (Bk. 1, Pt. 2, ch. 346); English translation by Thomas Johnes (third edition in 12 volumes, London, 1808), vol. iv, pp. 164-7, 185, 189.

47.   Details in D.L. Evans' article in *TSC*, as cited in note 42 above, pp. 71-73.

48.   Rhys (as cited in note 23 above, p.2) draws attention to the following entry in the *Record of Carnarvon*, p. 133, which is quoted by E. Owen (as cited in note 45 above, p.9): 'Gruff' Says libertenens praedicti principis de comitatu Angles' convictus fuit coram praefato justicario quod Conewey de sedicione super appello de eo quod adherens fuisset Owino Lawegogh inimico et proditori praedicti domini principis et de consilio praedicti Owyni ad mouendam guerram in Wallia contra praedictum dominum principem . . . '

49.   See Griffiths, pp. 159-160, and the section on Welsh prophetic poetry contributed to E. Owen's article, quoted in note 45 above, by J.H. Davies, pp. 81-100.

50.   Griffiths, pp. 159-160, and, with text, J.H. Davies and E. Owen, as cited in previous note, pp. 90-92. The poem was at first thought to refer to Owain Glyndŵr, but the description of 'Owain' as a sailor and the reference to the killing of his two uncles accord only with what is known of Owain Lawgoch.

51.   E. Owen, *op.cit.*, p. 17, refers to a payment of 100 francs and also quotes from the Issue Roll of the Exchequer dated 4 December [1378]: 'To John Lamb, an esquire from Scotland, because he lately killed Owynn de Gales, a rebel and enemy of the King in France . . . By writ of privy seal, &c., £20.'

52.   See Griffiths, p. 160, and J.H. Davies/E. Owen, *op.cit.* in notes 45/49 above, pp. 92-93.

53.   F. Jones, p. 42.

54.   *Cywyddau Iolo Goch ac eraill*, edited by Sir Ifor Williams, et.al., Cardiff, 1972, xvi, 33 (p.47); F. Jones, p. 170.

55.   F. Jones, p. 170.

56.   *Ibid*. On Richard II's recognition of Roger, see James Gairdner, *The Houses of Lancaster and York*, London, 1874, p. 56.

57.   *Chronicon Adae de Usk*, as cited in note 12 above, p. 71 (translation pp. 238-239).

58.   F. Jones, pp. 161-162.

59.   *Ibid.*, p. 171.

60.   Thomas Pennant, 'Of Owen Glyndwr'; Appendix vii to his *Tours in Wales*, edited by John Rhys, vol. 3 (Caernarvon, 1883), p.322.

61.   Ian Skidmore (*Owain Glyndŵr, Prince of Wales,*Swansea, 1978, p. 125) says: 'In keeping with his new dignity, Owain now assumed the trappings of royalty. He took a more impressive coat of arms to replace the dragon rampant under which he had fought as a rebel. On the bronze bosses of his horses' martingales were the four lions rampant counterchanged in gold and red, the ancient Royal arms of Gwynnedd'. Skidmore then quotes Adam of Usk's disapproving comment that Owain 'usurped the right of conquest and other marks of royalty'.

62.   *Red Book of Hergest*, col. 1053, 11.32-33; Griffiths, p. 135.

63.   F. Jones, p. 170.

Chapter 4: The Tudor Dragon and the Modern Symbol of the Welsh Nation

1. Quoted by H.T. Evans, p. 10.

2. See F. Jones, p. 173, who refers to British Museum Seals no. lxxx, 77 and 78. 'Supporters' to arms are figures of living creatures placed on either side of the shield, as though to hold it up.

3. Thomas Roberts and Ifor Williams, *The Poetical Works of Dafydd Nanmor*, Cardiff, 1923, p. 35, poem 13 (I ddau fab Owain Tudor o Fon), 11. 57ff; Draig velen, ar vyrr ennyd,/A draig wen a dery i [gyd]. /A gyfaulau'r ddraig velen/A ddyry [gwymp] i'r ddraig wen.

4. Text in Owen Jones, *Ceinion Llenyddiaeth Gymreig*, London, 1876, p. 220.

5. Quoted by H.T. Evans, p.8.

6. Text in *Gorchestion Beirdd Cymru*, edited by Rhys Jones, Shrewsbury, 1773, p. 177.

7. 'Os daw r anhap estronion/Jaspart a fag in ddragwn/Gwaed Bruttus happus yw hwn': *Brut*, 34-36, quoted by Garmon Jones, pp. 32f., 45.

8. On this, see Glanmor Williams, 'Prophecy, Poetry and Politics in Medieval and Tudor Wales', Chapter 3 of his *Religion, Language and Nationality in Wales*, Cardiff, 1979.

9. See H. Zimmer's historical survey, 'Der Pan-Keltismus in Grossbritannien und Irland', *Preussische Jahrbücher*, 92 (1898), 426-494, especially pp. 437-438.

10. Anglo (1961), p. 20.

11. Quoted by John Wynn of Gwydir, *History of the Gwydir Family*, with an introduction by John Ballinger, Cardiff, 1927, p. 28.

12. Garmon Jones, pp. 16-18.

13. Ian Skidmore, *Gwynedd*, London, 1986, p.82.

14. Full text of this letter of Henry's is given by John Wynn, *loc.cit.* in note 11 above.

15. Hugh Thomas, *A History of Wales, 1465-1660*, Cardiff, 1972, p. 23.

16. Edward Hall, *Chronicle Containing the History of England from Henry IV to Henry VIII*, edited by H. Ellis, London, 1809, p. 423.

17. Arthur H. Thomas and I.D. Thornley, *The Great Chronicle of London*, London, 1938, pp. 238-239.

18. Illustrations in *Banners, Standards and Badges from a Tudor Manuscript in the College of Arms*, with an introduction by Lord Howard de Walden; published by the De Walden Library, 1904, pp. 78, 80.

19. Glanmor Williams, *Henry Tudor and Wales*, Cardiff, 1985, p. 79.

20. Quoted by Anglo (1969), p. 49.

21. *Ibid*, p. 45.

22. *Ibid.*, p. 31.

23. Anglo (1961), p. 24n., quoting Humphrey Lloyd, *The History of Cambria*, edited by David Powel, 1584 (no place of publication indicated), p. 391.

24. 'Obtulit unum (draconem ex auro) in ecclesia primae sedis ecclesiae Wintoniae'; Geoffrey of Monmouth quoted by Wild (1963), p. 97, who also notes that, for Layamon too, this royal symbol is located at the episcopal seat of Winchester.

25. Anglo (1969), p. 55.

26. Anglo (1961), p. 39; F. Jones, p. 174.

27. F. Jones, *loc.cit.*

28. Anglo (1961), pp. 21-24.

29. See C.W. Scott-Giles, as cited above in note 35 to Chapter 1, p. 149.

30. H. Stanford London, *Royal Beasts*, East Knowle (Wilts.), 1956, p.46.

31. See the coloured illustration of Elizabeth's dragon in Guy C. Rothery, *Armorial Insignia of the Princes of Wales*, London, 1911, p. 70: cf. F. Jones, p. 175.

32. F. Jones, pp. 174f.

33. Queen Anne used two dragons on her seal for Chester; and 'a lion and a dragon support the royal arms on James I's and Charles I's seals for the Court of Wards, on James' seal for the

same court in Ireland and on William IV's seal for the Court of King's Bench': H.S. London, as cited in note 30 above, p. 45. He adds other examples.

34. Anglo (1961), p. 40.

35. Wild (1963), pp. 99-100.

36. Skidmore, as cited in note 13 above, p. 82.

37. Hugh Thomas as cited in note 15 above, pp. 105-106.

38. W. Ogwen Williams, *Tudor Gwynedd. The Tudor Age in the Principality of Wales*, Caernarvonshire Historical Society, 1958.

39. Wagner, as cited above in note 38 to Chapter 3. F. Jones (p. 172) notes that the dragon 'never became popular in Welsh heraldry and with one exception is never found in Cymric shields until the present century. None of the numerous landed families who derived from the Five Royal and Fifteen Noble Tribes, and from other great chieftains, adopted the dragon as a heraldic charge'.

40. John E. Lloyd notes (in his *Owen Glendower*, Oxford, 1931, p. 138) that when Glyndŵr fled from the besiegers of Harlech Castle and then finally disappeared, he 'left behind him in the castle one little personal relic which has recently been unearthed in the course of excavations, viz. a gilt bronze boss from a set of horse harness, bearing the four lions rampant which he had assumed as prince of Wales'. Cf. *Ibid.*, p. 84.

41. Lewis Glyn Cothi, *Poetical Works*, Oxford, 1837, p. 481, 11.15-16.

42. Details in Kenneth O. Morgan, *Rebirth of a Nation. Wales 1880-1980*, Oxford and New York, 1981, pp. 94ff and passim. Also chapter 17 ('The Growth of National Consciousness') in David Williams, *A History of Modern Wales*, second edition, London, 1977.

43. Gerald R. Morgan gives census figures from 1891 to 1961, recording a decline in numbers of Welsh speakers from 54.4 to 26 per cent of the population. He notes that 'one consequence of the decline of the language has been a sharpened awareness of its value' (pp. 28-30 of his book with the significant title *The Dragon's Tongue*, Cardiff, 1966),

44.   F. Jones, p. 176.

45.   H.S. London, *loc.cit.*, in note 30 above. Cf. F. Jones pp. 163-164. He says that the 'banner of Wales' carried at royal funerals, up to that of Queen Mary in 1695, most likely displayed the lions of Gwynedd; and that subsequently these lions "disappeared from royal heraldry until 1911, when they were placed, by order of King George V, in an inescutcheon on the arms of Edward, Prince of Wales, being then specifically denoted as 'the arms of Wales'".

46.   F. Jones, p. 178.

47.   On the 1890's, see H. Zimmer, as cited in note 9 above, p. 480. On the petition to George V, see F. Jones, p, 196.

48.   Glyn Jones, *The Dragon has Two Tongues. Essays on Anglo-Welsh Writers and Writing*, London, 1968.

Index